Oyama
The Legend, The Legacy

Oyama   The Legend, The Legacy

Michael J. Lorden

SPECIAL INTEREST PUBLICATIONS

265 S. Anita Drive, Ste. 120
Orange, CA 92868

Library of Congress Catalog Number: 00-130302
ISBN: 1-892515-24-5

Distributed by:
Unique Publications
265 S. Anita Drive, Ste. 120
Orange, CA 92868

First edition
05 04 03 02 01 00 99 98 97 1 3 5 7 9 10 8 6 4 2

Printed in the United States of America

Book design by Patrick Gross
Format by George Foon
Edited by Mark V. Wiley
Cover concept by Stuart Olson

To Jennifer,
for your patience,
understanding,
and love.

Contents

1. Godhand—The Legend 1

2. The Beginning 15

3. Honbu (Headquarters) 29

4. Oyama and Bushido 45

5. Kyokushin—The Ultimate Truth 57

6. Osu 65

7. Training 75

8. Young Lions of Oyama 89

9. Jissen Kumite (Full-Contact Fighting) 101

10. Hyakunin Kumite (100-Man Fighting) 115

11. World Champions 129

12. Kyokushinkai Ambassadors 147

13. The Legacy 153

Chronology of Mas Oyama and Kyokushinkai 163

References 171

About the Author 173

Chapter 1

Godhand—The Legend

reparations on my side and for the filming were completed. The proposed place was the Yawata coast of Tateyama in Chiba Prefecture. On the day of the filming, upon looking at the bull the movie company had brought, I was frightened. It was a large bull weighing about 1,250 pounds with a horn ten inches long and three inches around the base. To tell the truth, I was quite uneasy, but since I could not very well withdraw, I resolved to proceed. Newspapermen, magazine reporters, together with the filming crew caused quite a stir in the quiet fishing hamlet. Topics among the spectators were, "Can he really break the horn with his bare hand? I can't believe it. Isn't he lightheaded?" They were in doubt to the outcome of this event. Unfortunately, the duel was postponed because of rain.

"Well, you are lucky, sir. Your life was extended for one day," joked a newspaperman. I was, however, far from a joking mood and held a telegram sent from my only daughter, which read, "Good luck, Daddy!"

"The next day proved to be a fine one and there were thousands of spectators. I wore short pants tightened with a wide leather belt and, of course, no protection on my hands. Spectators raised a big cry of excitement. "Don't lose," they shouted! Standing by the seashore, I raised my hands high and closed my eyes to take a posture free from all thoughts. When I opened my eyes, the thousands of people, the four movie projectors equipped with telescopes, fear for the bull—all these things had vanished from my consciousness. Now the huge black bull was released from a rope. I swiftly dodged its attack right and left and finally grasped it by the horns. I tried to twist it down to the ground, but the 1,250 pound bull, spreading its legs, refused to budge. Instead, the press of the bull forced my feet to stick in the sand. At last my hands slipped off the horns because of perspiration and the enraged bull rushed at me with terrible force. Before the filming of the event, I had been asked by the movie director to battle for about ten minutes, but I had no reserve to do so. If worst comes to worst I would be thrust to death. We kept up the bloody struggle. Suddenly I missed my footing and fell on my back. I felt my position to be precarious, but it was too late to raise myself up and the bull, with a low snort, made a thrust at me. Though I recovered quickly, my skin was torn from abdomen to breast. The blood flowed, but I felt no pain. Instantly grabbing the horns with my hands I twisted its neck right and left with all my might. The bull, shaking *its horns right and left, tried to slip off my hands. Gradually I felt my opponent becoming tired. The moment I noticed this, I twisted with all my might. When it toppled down into the sand making a heavy thud, I jumped in quickly to grip the horns firmly with my hands. Its large abdomen was beating thunderously and both the bull and I were covered with perspiration and sand. While my opponent tried to get up, I pressed down trying to keep it from doing so. I concentrated on my right* shuto *(knife-hand). With a yell I struck the base of the horn. The bull groaned; its horn, broken at the root, was hanging down from its forehead. I pulled the horn from the forehead and unconsciously held it high over my head. Suddenly the stir of the spectators like a distant thunder reached my ears. I had conquered the bull. At last I could realize my long-cherished desire. I was moved to tears. The death struggle with the bull had lasted thirty-five minutes. I felt it neither long nor short—I simply fought with all my might . . ."*

The above narration is Mas Oyama's account of his thoughts, reflections, fears, and triumphs during his first life-or-death ordeal with a bull. One would think that after pitting one's strength against bulls and pushing oneself to the maximum of physical endurance during isolation in the mountains, this would be quite the adequate test for an individual.

But not for Oyama.

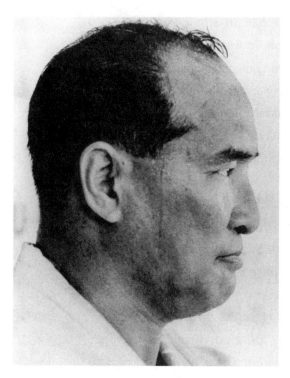

Profile of Mas Oyama.

He wanted to test the practical application of his karate. He believed that it was essential to train with an opponent with contact in the same manner as boxers. In 1952 he accepted an invitation to come to the United States in a challenge to face other fighters. For one year Oyama accepted two-hundred-and-seventy challenges. He fought boxers, wrestlers, bouncers, and anyone who issued a challenge. He was undefeated. The majority of the matches were won with a single punch. Oyama was now being referred to as "The Godhand" by everyone. In Japan he was being proclaimed: *"Ichi geki, hissatsu!"*—"One strike, certain death."

A tradition within the Japanese culture is to bestow nicknames upon famous individuals. One such nickname bestowed upon Mas Oyama was "The Godhand." Westerners not familiar with Japanese culture and tradition may find this reference inappropriate or somewhat over-dramatic. However, in 1955 even Western journalists were using "The Godhand" when referring to Mas Oyama in their articles of his exploits. This was due in part after witnessing Oyama's incredible feats of *tameshiwari* (breaking) and fighting, during exhibitions given in the United States and South America. For nearly fifty years, fifteen million plus members of Oyama's worldwide Kyokushin karate organization witnessed this man's incredible feats. Whether from the power of his strikes, the strength of his handshake, his remarkable teachings, or through the teachings of the instructors and branch chiefs that Oyama produced, everyone associated with him knew that this esoteric name was not inappropriate. Growing up, there were many people and experiences that affected this enigmatic man. Although we do not know all of the details involving his formative years, we do have a fairly good outline.

Masutatsu (Mas) Oyama, was born Yong-I Choi, on July 27, 1923, in the tiny village of Wa-Ryongri Yong-chi Myonchul Na Do, in South Korea. His family, considered aristocrats, belonged to the Yangban-clan. His father, Sun Hyang, was the mayor of Kinje, a town near the village where Yong-I Choi was born. As a young child, nine years of age, Oyama began studying southern Chinese kempo under the instruction of Mr. Yi, an employee on the estate owned by Oyama's father. Oyama was also an avid reader and was deeply affected and moved after reading the biography of Otto von Bismark (1815–98) the Prussian Chancellor (1871–90) of the German empire. Bismark, Oyama read, was instrumental in unifying Germany in a span of only two-to-three years, making it a nation powerful enough to control most of Europe.

The philosophy of Bismark made such a strong impression on Oyama that he decided he wanted to be the Bismark of the Orient. With great aspirations Oyama somehow felt his destiny was in Japan and he left Korea at the age of fifteen.

Alone in Tokyo, the young Korean wandered aimlessly throughout the city seeking refuge in local boarding houses, only to be turned away at each location. Feeling unwanted in this alien country, Oyama began to regret leaving Korea and wondered if he had made a terrible mistake. As luck would have it, the young Choi met a family of Korean origin that sympathized with their fellow countryman. They offered to rent him a room in their home.

It was at this time that Choi followed the customary procedure of Korean immigrants to Japan of changing their names to Japanese, hoping to be better accepted into society. In honor of the family that befriended him, Choi selected the name Oyama. From this point on he would no longer be known as Yong-I Choi, but as Masutatsu Oyama. The Korean Oyama family he was now living with had two sons, Shigeru and Yasuhiko. Both Shigeru and Yasuhiko would later become martial art students under Mas Oyama and go on to become two of the most prominent and famous members of the Kyokushinkaikan.

In 1938, at the young age of fifteen, Oyama wanted to serve the country he now called home and therefore joined Japan's Yamanashi Youth Air Force Academy with the intentions of becoming a pilot. In September of this same year, Oyama became a student of Shotokan karate founder Gichin Funakoshi, at Takushoku University. Funakoshi, a school teacher from Okinawa, was credited with introducing karate to Japan. It is this man whom Oyama later would refer to as his true karate teacher. Throughout the years Oyama always spoke highly of Funakoshi, remarking in later recollections of his gentle yet overwhelming presence. Oyama went on to say that of the many things he learned from Funakoshi, *kata* (formal exercises) was the most important.

By the age of eighteen, Oyama had earned the rank of *nidan* (second level black belt) in karate. Oyama was still very much a patriot and was always volunteering for special military duty. On one assignment to an airfield near Tokyo, a confrontation provoked by an officer resulted in Oyama striking the officer. Although found innocent due to the provocation on the part of the officer, Oyama was ordered transferred to an area in the Pacific. However, the war was just ending and, lucky for Oyama, the transfer was halted. This luck had an ironic twist for Oyama because it also meant that his driving quest to serve his new country was now over. The announcement that Japan had surrendered WWII quickly ended Oyama's military career. The stress of losing his career and the dishonor he felt for his adopted country losing the war created great—almost unbearable—stress in Oyama's life.

Oyama's stress turned into trouble that seemed to plague him wherever he went. Disheartened and doubting himself, Oyama became engaged in a series of events that would lead to one mistake after another. Oyama was a very large and strong individual, but he was naive to the ways of the world. His size and naivete were ideal characteristics for the gangsters operating the various black market enterprises throughout Japan to exploit. These syndicate gangsters enlisted Oyama's assistance with promises of easy money. Of course the type of assistance the gangsters sought was brute force and violence against anyone who crossed them. It was through this association with the gangster element that resulted in Oyama being arrested and incarcerated for six months.

After his release from jail, Oyama felt the need to redeem himself, and the only redemption he knew was to immerse himself in the martial arts and train as hard as he could. Already a nidan rank in karate from Funakoshi, Oyama wanted more than rank from his martial arts training.

Although practice of the martial arts was prohibited at the time by the occupying forces in Japan, there were covert places one could go to train. It was only necessary to know the language and have a formal introduction to the instructor.

Oyama found someone Korean like himself by the name of Nei-Chu So. Not only was So Korean but he was also from the same province as Oyama. Nei-Chi So was a practitioner of the Goju-ryu style of karate. Goju-ryu, founded by Chojun Miyagi in 1930, was being carried on in Japan by Gogen Yamaguchi, nicknamed "The Cat." Yamaguchi commonly acknowledged that Nei-Chu So was one of his best students. Oyama quickly resumed his martial arts training under So, and a strong bond was formed between the two. So, a great philosopher and strong in character, possessed even stronger spiritual convictions. Oyama would not only learn Goju-ryu from So, but would also be sanctified by him into the Buddhist faith of the Nichiren sect. It was So who inspired Oyama to make karate his life-long dedication, propelling him to face his own challenges and develop his own achievements and victories. At the same time he began his training with So, Oyama earnestly took up the practice of judo as well. After four years of training, he received his *yondan* (fourth level black belt) ranking in judo.

Oyama liked to attend the local dance competitions in the area in order to socialize and relax after his martial arts training. It was at one such dance event that Oyama came to the aid of a female who was being accosted by a local trouble maker. When Oyama intervened, the trouble maker, a tall Japanese suspected of several homicides, became enraged and produced a knife. Taunting Oyama, the trouble maker made continuous slashing movements through the air in front of Oyama's face with the knife and then lunged towards Oyama. Oyama blocked the attack and delivered a forceful punch to the head of the assailant, killing him instantly. Because of eyewitness accounts of the incident, Oyama was ruled by the courts as justified in using self-defense. However, the impact of the tragedy devastated Oyama. To kill a man with a single blow was so overwhelming to Oyama that he decided to give up his martial arts training. Learning that the man he killed had a wife and children on a farm in the Kanto area near Tokyo, Oyama went to the farm and worked there for several months. He did not leave until the widow assured him that she was financially capable of maintaining the farm and that she did not hold Oyama responsible for the death of her husband.

This became the turning point in Oyama's life. His Goju-ryu instructor, Nei-Chu So, advised him to go away, to train his body and soul and to give karate a chance to control his life. Oyama, lacking direction and a goal wondered if karate was a realistic goal. Would karate training give him the much needed control of his physical strength as well as mental discipline? If karate would provide these traits, then he would have to give himself completely to the training. He realized it would be a long, hard journey. He was determined to succeed on this quest.

In 1948 Mas Oyama, taking with him only his books and the basic necessities for cooking, began an arduous training regimen atop Mt. Minobu in Chiba Prefecture. Mt. Minobu is the same place where the famous seventeenth century samurai, Miyamoto Musashi, received inspiration for Nito-ryu, his celebrated double sword system. To Oyama, this was the ideal place to train and be inspired in the same tradition as his idol Musashi. Of the

Mas Oyama in anza (seated) posture prior to meditation at honbu.

books Oyama took with him on this journey, none were more important than the collection on Musashi, by Yoshikawa. For eighteen months, isolated in the mountains, Oyama tested himself against nature's elements with such scenarios as training and meditating under icy waterfalls, performing countless jumps over bushes and boulders, and using trees and rocks as *makiwara* (striking aide) to condition his hands, feet, and legs. He would begin training at five in the morning, running up the steep slopes. Using large rocks as weights, he would lift them hundreds of times to increase his strength. In addition, he performed kata a minimum of one hundred times each day as well as hundreds upon thousands of repetitions of *kihon* (basic techniques), continuously pushing himself to the limits of human endurance. At the conclusion of his daily training, he would read various Buddhist writings and sit in *zazen* (seated meditation) and meditate. It was also at this time that Oyama began to contemplate the idea of the circle and point for his karate. He also began visualizing himself defeating a bull with his bare hands. If he could get strong enough and powerful enough that he was able to defeat a bull with his karate, he would become famous. But it wasn't fame he was after. The fame, he thought, would be a tool. If he could attract interest from others, he could enlighten them on the strengths and virtues of karate and he would succeed not only in his goal of mastering karate, but of instructing others in the way of karate as well.

After eighteen months of solitude, Oyama returned from the mountains. Shortly after his return from the mountain training, the first karate tournament since the end of World War II was held in Japan. Oyama competed in this All Japan Karate

Tournament held at the Maruyama Kaikan in Kyoto and emerged victorious—the tournament's first champion. But Oyama was an intense young man and still was not satisfied with his achievement. He still felt that something was lacking in his martial arts and that he had not truly reached his full potential. Oyama returned to the mountains for another year of grueling fourteen-hour training days.

To this day, there is no other person who has undertaken such a training regimen within the martial arts. After this final isolation and training period, Oyama returned to civilization ready to apply all that he had learned. It was at this time Oyama decided to apply his karate expertise in a life and death battle. A conflict that would set man against beast.

Chapter 2

The Beginning

O yama's reputation as a karate practitioner was spreading rapidly. His victory at the All Japan Tournament and his isolated mountain training were reported throughout the country. News of his exploits reached the United States and in April of 1952 Oyama was invited by the Chicago Pro Wrestlers Association to participate in bouts in Chicago. Oyama decided his battle against a bull would have to wait and he accepted their invitation. On opening night in Chicago, Oyama faced three pro wrestlers and was victorious in all three matches. His accomplishments were being featured in newspapers and such notable magazines as *Look,* *Time,* and *Life.* What was only to be a short tour in Chicago, grew into a ten-month tour of thirty-two states, Canada, Mexico, and Cuba. Oyama would face opponents of various styles of unarmed combat. He defeated all challengers, many with just a single blow, and demonstrated amazing and breath-taking tameshiwari (a widely misunderstood concept that is demonstrated by breaking or smashing bricks, stones, and blocks with the extremities). If the time was ever right for Oyama to realize his goal of fighting a bull and furthering the position of karate, it was now.

After his return to Japan, Oyama organized a bare-handed dual against a bull. His encounter and ensuing defeat of the bull is described in the opening paragraph in the previous chapter.

Oyama would face forty-seven bulls throughout his career, killing four of them instantly with a single strike. During one of these bouts in Mexico in 1957, Oyama was gored so badly that he was hospitalized for six months. This grave incident did not deter him from continuing his engagements. For the next few years he opposed several more bulls, defeating them all. Even though all of the bulls were earmarked for the slaughter-house prior to facing Oyama, there were still many complaints from various animal rights groups. Abiding by their wishes, Oyama ended these life-and-death encounters against bulls, thus concluding this phase of his karate dream and beginning another.

Oyama started his first *dojo* in the year 1953 outdoors in a field in Mejiro, Tokyo. His training assistant was Kenji Masushima. Many of Oyama's first students were from other styles of karate who came to Oyama for the hard training. Oyama was not only a firm believer in extreme physical conditioning, he also believed that for practical applications of karate, the students needed to understand the limitations

Mas Oyama performing shuto uchi (knifehand strike) at honbu.

of certain techniques as well as the limitations of various other styles. *Kumite* (fighting) sessions during training were *jissen* (full-contact, sans protective equipment) in order for students to appreciate and learn the techniques that worked versus those that did not. Due to the intensity and severity of the training, the dropout rate was quite high. However, Oyama continued and over the next three years succeeded in building a strong student base.

Oyama opened his first official dojo in 1956. It was located in a small building behind Rikkyo University, not far from where he would eventually build the *honbu* (headquarters). It was also in 1956 that Oyama chose the name Kyokushin for the karate style that he developed. He chose the name Kyokushin because of the proverb; *"One becomes a beginner after one thousand days of practice and an expert after ten thousand days of practice,"* which he defined as "the ultimate truth." Therefore, Oyama decided his karate organization would be known as *Kyokushinkai,* or Society of the Ultimate Truth. Oyama now had other assistant instructors, including Eiji Yasuda, Masami Ishibashi, Ken Minamoto, as well as Kenji Masushima. Within one year Oyama's total student enrollment grew to seven hundred despite the intense training and full-contact fighting.

During the next ten years, Oyama continued to build his organization and began his own world-wide crusade, professing at every opportunity, through whatever means available, the importance of karate. He believed that his ideology of karate, coupled with powerful Zen influences, were capable of supporting world peace. Oyama's commitment to world peace through the practice of karate was unwavering. He would not permit anyone or anything to cause him to deviate from his quest. At last, Oyama seemed to be circling back to the idealism of his youth when he was so inspired by Bismark.

Because of his compassion for humanity and strong convictions, Oyama never neglected an opportunity to extol the virtues of karate. Like a missionary, he traveled the world spreading the word of karate. Wherever and whenever fighting challenges were made, Oyama would accept them and was never once defeated. One of the more significant challenges he accepted was against the welterweight Thai boxing champion known as "The Black Cobra." Oyama became the first karate man to ever defeat a Thai boxer. Again, the name Oyama was spoken with high regard in the karate world because of this victory.

Knowing that it was impossible for him alone to reach all parts of the world, Oyama enlisted the aid of his top students. He realized that if his karate was to be accepted worldwide, it would take more than just demonstrations and fights. Oyama then began sending his top students to various countries. These were not temporary assignments. These students, believing so strongly in Oyama and his karate, were agreeing to leave their homeland of Japan and set up permanent residences in unfamiliar countries. Their mission was to open schools and teach Kyokushin karate. This was an undeniably difficult task since until this time, karate was all but unheard of outside of Japan, especially in the Western world. Mas Oyama is credited with being the first to introduce karate to the Western world. In his book, *The Kyokushin Way: Mas Oyama's Philosophy,* he writes the following:

"I must say a word to clarify the nature of the karate boom that is sweeping the world and to explain its origin. The assumption that certain action motion pictures stimulated worldwide interest in karate is ridiculous. The actor who starred in those motion pictures was a student of a student of a student of mine. He was not a true karate man, but an actor. Nonetheless, he had great respect for me and for Kyokushin karate and is said to have kept a large photograph of me in his room.

"The karate boom did not start with him, and it did not start in Japan. In fact, Japan has been among the last nations of the world to feel its influence. Karate's popularity on a global scale started when I made tours of the United States. giving exhibitions from one end of the country to the other. Gradually I published books on the subject in English, French, German, Dutch, and ten other languages and opened karate training halls in fifty-five nations. The renown of Kyokushin karate grew so great that young men in other lands, assuming that all my countrymen are karate experts, sometimes approach any oriental person and ask for karate instructions. Unfortunately, this popularity has had an adverse effect in the form of many training halls falsely operated under my name without my permission. The men involved in this kind of thing usually have done no more than read my books; and, as anyone knows, karate cannot be learned from books alone.

*"Though I killed bulls with my bare hands and chal-
lenged all comers from the national karate association, in
the days immediately after the end of World War II, men
of the martial arts enjoyed little esteem in this country. For
that reason I traveled in other lands showing the power of
karate and winning many students and friends. It was
only much later that Kyokushin karate—that is, global
karate—entered Japan in a form very different from that of
any of the pre-war Japanese schools. I repeat that it was
my work, and not the popularized fame of a motion picture actor, that brought karate international fame and
popularity."*

The first Kyokushin school to open outside of Japan was in
Hawaii in 1957. In 1952, during Mas Oyama's U.S. tour, he
visited Hawaii to perform a demonstration. Many of those in
attendance that day were practitioners of various forms of
martial arts themselves, and not so receptive of an outsider
demonstrating another martial art. They were also somewhat
reluctant to attend, believing that the demonstration would
be similar to hundreds of others seen in the past. Oyama
began the demonstration by performing a kata. Immediately
some of those in attendance began to leave. They were quick
to presume that their assumptions were justified and that
they would be witnessing the same old thing. They assumed
incorrectly. Oyama, seeing some of the spectators leave and
sensing disappointment in others, quickly changed strategy.

Mas Oyama performing nukite (spearhand).

Usually saving his tameshiwari exhibitions until last, he abandoned his plan and began tameshiwari immediately.

Now, Oyama's remarkable feats of breaking are unmatched even to this day, for in addition to snapping the horn from a bull with his powerful *shuto-uchi* (knifehand-strike) he was also able to break three bricks, placed one on top of another. He could easily smash through thirty roofing tiles with a single punch. Large stones, blocks of ice, and wood were no match for Oyama's strength. Those individuals assisting Oyama during his breaking demonstrations were often covered with blankets or carpets so they would not be injured from flying debris. During one such demonstration, several students were holding a stack of wood vertically for Oyama to punch. He punched with so much force that his fist continued through, striking one of the holders and breaking the student's ribs.

Whenever Oyama broke bricks, concrete blocks, or wood piled atop each other, he never utilized devices that allowed space between each item. These "spacers," as they are known, greatly increase the ease of breaking by lessening the density. Needless to say, Oyama's breaking astonished those in attendance that day in Hawaii and gained the respect of all the other martial artists who had gathered there to witness the demonstration.

One young man in attendance who was so duly astonished was Bobby Lowe. Lowe's father was a kung-fu instructor and had been instructing his son accordingly in a Chinese martial art. At the age of twenty-three, Lowe held black belt rankings in judo, kempo, and aikido. However, he still was not completely satisfied with his martial arts and he sought out Oyama after the demonstration. For the next two weeks, Bobby Lowe trained daily with Oyama. He was overwhelmed by Oyama's abilities. For the next several months, after Oyama left, Lowe continued to practice the Kyokushin techniques Oyama taught him. Six months later, Oyama returned to Hawaii to visit Lowe and instructed him regularly for another three weeks. Before he left Hawaii, Oyama invited Bobby Lowe to come to Japan and train. Bobby Lowe would later accept that offer.

Mas Oyama had been contemplating a program in which students would live at the honbu and immerse themselves in the study of Kyokushin karate. When Bobby Lowe accepted Oyama's offer to come to Japan, Oyama put his plan into effect and Lowe became the first *uchi-deshi* (live-in student) of Kyokushin and Mas Oyama.

Bobby Lowe trained under the direction of Mas Oyama for eighteen months. Upon returning to Hawaii, Lowe continued to train in the Kyokushin style. It would take several more trips to Japan for training, but eventually Lowe was ready and, in 1957, he opened the first Oyama Kyokushin karate school outside of Japan. Shihan Bobby Lowe, now in his 70s, is a 7th *dan* in Kyokushin and continues to instruct at his Honolulu dojo. Mas Oyama would often refer to Lowe as his brother and Lowe remained a trusted friend to Oyama until Oyama's passing.

Many of Oyama's senior students not only acted as diplomats for Kyokushin in foreign countries, they too, like Oyama, accepted various challenges. And like Oyama's, these challenges would help spread the power and discipline of Kyokushin worldwide. But since Oyama's defeat of the "The Black Cobra," no other practitioners of various styles of karate could repeat Oyama's victory and defeat the Thai boxers.

Thai boxers were renowned for their powerful shin and knee kicks, as well as their extensive punching arsenal. Like Oyama, they realized the necessity for training with contact.

This realistic form of training is unheard of in most other styles of martial art. Instead, other styles train the student to stop their techniques just short of their intended target. The many defeats of the karate practitioners at the hands of Thai boxers demonstrated that this form of training is not only unrealistic but unsuccessful. Following in the footsteps of Oyama, a five-man contingent from Oyama's headquarters in Japan traveled to Thailand to accept the challenge of the Thai boxers in 1964. These Kyokushin fighters were, like Oyama, victorious and returned to Japan with the world kickboxing championship title.

Of the five men from Kyokushin karate who traveled to Thailand in 1964, none was more impressive than Tadashi Nakamura. Nakamura began studying Kyokushin under Oyama in 1952 and became the youngest individual in Japan to receive the *shodan* (1st level black belt) ranking of the Kyokushinkai-kan. By the time he was nineteen, Nakamura attained the rank of nidan and was appointed chief instructor for Kyokushin at the U.S. military base, Camp Zama, near Tokyo. Years later he was appointed chief instructor at the Kyokushinkai headquarters in Tokyo. In 1966 Oyama sent Nakamura to the United States as chairman of the North American Kyokushinkai Organization. Nakamura, now chairman of his own organization, World Seido Karate, continued training under Oyama until the mid-1970s receiving his 7th dan from Oyama.

Mas Oyama used every means available in order to expand
the world of Kyokushin. Hundreds of newspaper and magazine articles were written about him. There were documentary
films, movies, and even a comic book published in Japan on
his exploits. He published several books on Kyokushin
karate. His first book *What is Karate?*, projected to sell only
5,000 copies, sold more than 500,000 copies worldwide.
Oyama continued to write and publish books about
Kyokushin karate. Many of these books would be published
worldwide in various languages. Some of the more popular of
these are: *This is Karate* (referred to as the Bible of Karate),
Advanced Karate, and *The Kyokushin Way*, which details Mas
Oyama's philosophy. Oyama continued to travel extensively
throughout the world lecturing, teaching, and demonstrating.
His 1958 visit to the U.S. and month-long instruction to the
FBI was of great value to the law enforcement community.
His students continued to relocate in foreign countries and
establish Kyokushin dojos. Oyama would eventually build his
Kyokushin into a worldwide organization with a membership
exceeding fifteen million. He would preside over and manage
this organization from his headquarters in Japan. The honbu
would be known as the Kyokushinkaikan.

Chapter 3

Honbu
(Headquarters)

*J*n 1964 construction was complete and Oyama officially opened his honbu in the Ikebukuro section of Tokyo. This multi-story building housed two dojos, receptionist area, an apartment-sized living quarter, Mas Oyama's office, staff area, and a basement level where dressing rooms and storage facilities were located. The building was unique for that time in that it was utilized solely for the instruction of karate and the day-to-day operation of the Kyokushin organization. Another unique aspect of the structure was that Oyama owned it. All other karate styles in Japan at the time could only afford to lease buildings for the use of dojos.

Prior to the construction of the honbu in Ikebukuro, Oyama conducted his karate classes in a building behind Rikkyo University that was also being used as a ballet studio. At that time Oyama's eldest daughter was studying ballet at the studio. One day after a ballet class, her teacher approached her and asked if she would bring her father by for a meeting. When Oyama arrived for the meeting, he was told by the teacher that *Yakuza* (Japanese organized crime) were causing problems. The teacher went on to explain that due to Oyama's reputation as a strong karate practitioner he would like Oyama to use his facility for training. It was obvious that the ballet teacher hoped Oyama's presence would deter the Yakuza from further harassment. Oyama accepted the offer and thus the beginning of the first dojo was established.

During this start-up stage of the dojo, times were extremely tough for Oyama. He and his family were forced to move from their home in Mejiro after being deceived and cheated by certain individuals. They moved to the Itabashi section of Tokyo. The meager income Oyama generated from teaching karate forced him and his family to eat nothing but sweet potatoes for several days in a row. However, Oyama was determined to succeed in establishing a strong karate following. His enthusiasm was shared by his wife, Chiyako, who gave full support to her husband.

During this stressful time, the moods of Oyama's wife and his children were low. One day he and his wife were in Ikebukuro when they unexpectedly came upon a piece of real estate for sale. Oyama proposed the idea of purchasing the land and building a home even though their financial resources were lacking and the proposition seemed hopeless. It was at this moment that Oyama had the idea to write a book about karate and reasoned that he could use the money from the book as a down payment on the land.

Oyama soon realized that although his material for a book was plentiful, finding someone willing to publish it was another matter. After several rejections he and his wife began to think the book project and their hopes of buying the land was a dead-end.

With their hopes quickly dwindling, Oyama and his wife were advised to try a publisher who specialized in overseas markets. After the initial meeting between Oyama and Nichibo Shuppan, the president of the publishing company, Mr. Shuppan agreed to publish the book. When asked by his associates why he agreed to publish Oyama's book, Mr. Shuppan replied that Oyama did not flaunt himself, nor did he bestow tributes upon the company to win approval as so many others have done. Mr. Shuppan also said that not once did Oyama ask anything about money. The release of *This is Karate* was a major success in the United States. The royalties from the book allowed Oyama and his wife the opportunity to purchase the land in Ikebukuro.

While the construction of Oyama's home was still in the planning stages, the course Oyama and Chiyako were following would take a sudden change in direction. After completion of karate training one evening at the ballet studio, a student commented: "It would be nice to have a shower." Until then, Oyama had not even thought of building a dojo, but when he mentioned the student's comment to his wife, the decision was made. Their new home would wait. Mrs. Oyama supported the idea of building a dojo. Thus, the beginning of the honbu.

When construction of the honbu began, Mrs. Oyama would visit the site daily to watch the progress. She was very happy. However, it was not all happiness and joy, as problems abounded. Construction would come to a halt when funds for materials became scarce and then resume when more royalties rolled in from sales of the book. Now during those days, Sosai (founder) Mas Oyama and his family lived in a small apartment nearby, but with all their money going to construction, they were unable to pay their rent. Fearing eviction, Sosai Oyama and Chiyako advised their landlord of their financial situation and pleaded with him to allow them to live in the apartment, promising to pay as soon as it was possible. Amazingly, the landlord agreed to let them stay.

It was nearly two years before the construction of honbu was completed. Oyama acquired the assistance of several friends to help with the move into the honbu, and a party was held that evening for everyone who helped and for his students. Mrs. Oyama ordered refreshments for everyone, who were gathered in the basement celebrating the new honbu, when suddenly the president of the construction company approached Oyama, advising him that he could not allow Oyama and his family to move in until all his debts were paid.

Speechless, Sosai left the building. Mrs. Oyama would later recall that she could not imagine how Sosai must have felt at that moment. Oyama sought out several of his friends for support, but to no avail. Alone, Oyama walked the streets and contemplated his predicament. A car approached and the occupant called out: "Oyama, it's me!" Oyama recognized the man as Mr. Mori, a recent member of Parliament. At Mori's request they proceeded to his residence. Once there, Mori told Oyama the following story:

> *"When I was defeated in the first election, I believed I had failed. I was devastated and contemplated suicide. I thought of you, Oyama, and what you had accomplished. It was then I decided to try harder for the next election."*

When Mr. Mori noticed the somber mood of Oyama, he asked what was troubling him. After Sosai explained his financial dilemma, Mori, without hesitation, assembled the funds Oyama needed. Oyama returned to the honbu and paid the construction company president the balance due. The planned party then began.

The Kyokushin honbu, under the tutelage of Mas Oyama, was home to some of the most intense and demanding karate training undertaken throughout the world. Many of the initial cadre of students at the honbu came from other styles of karate. They came to receive the full-contact training for which Oyama had become known. Some of these students continued their training under their instructors of the other styles as well. This simultaneous training in two distinctly different schools of thought caused problems. In some instances, students would train with Oyama, then attend classes at their original schools. It was at these other schools during fighting training that these students would overpower and injure the other students with their Kyokushin training. Soon they were being reprimanded by their instructors and being dismissed from the schools. Some schools began sending groups of students to Oyama's honbu, issuing challenges. Because of this, Oyama posted students at the doors to stand guard and prevent such scenarios. To this day, students remain on guard at the doors of the honbu.

Many of Japan's top karate fighters came out of the Kyokushin honbu. The top-ranking and most knowledgeable instructors of the Kyokushinkai received their extensive training under Oyama. Four of the more prominent and recognized karate instructors in the martial arts world—Steve Arneil, Tadashi Nakamura, and the Oyama brothers, Shigeru and Yasuhiko (no relation to Mas Oyama)—were former students and instructors.

Many foreign students have traveled to Japan annually to train at the honbu under Oyama, as well as heads-of-state, royalty, and entertainment personalities. Dulph Lundgren, of action-movie fame is a European full-contact karate champion and Kyokushin stylist who received training at honbu. Another name synonymous with the motion picture industry is Sean Connery, who trained at the honbu to utilize Kyokushin's realistic applications in preparation for the movie *You Only Live Twice*. Many of Oyama's students were featured in the film. For his contribution to the martial arts world, depicting real karate in the movie, Mas Oyama presented Sean Connery with an honorary Kyokushin certification.

Branch Chiefs, those authorized by Oyama to establish schools outside of Japan and instruct in the teachings of Kyokushin and certify students, return regularly to the honbu to receive training. Here, under the careful watch of Oyama and his senior instructors, these branch chiefs receive advanced training, as well as work on maintaining their own Kyokushin skills. It is also at the honbu, after several yearly trips, that the branch chiefs, when eligible, undergo promotion examinations.

Entering the main dojo of the honbu, despite its age, one
perceives a clean and well-maintained facility. The respect
that has been bestowed upon the dojo by the thousands
upon thousands of students who have trained there is evident from the moment one steps onto its floor. The hard-
wood floor is smooth and polished from the countless
maneuverings by the students upon it. To the front, encom-
passing the entire width of the dojo, is the *shinza* (shrine).
This is a place that stands out from the rest of the dojo.
Tokens of special importance adorn the shinza. To this
domain, respect is given. It is the focal point of the dojo,
where the spirit of the dojo begins and ends.

For many people, the role of the shinza may be equated to a
mascot of a school or team, or the flag of a country. People
rally around a mascot or flag as a sign of solidarity. The sym-
bol represents the spirit of the school, team, or country. This
same spirit holds true for the shinza of a dojo. The shinza
has no religious connotations, but serves as a reminder to all
students, seniors, and instructors of their commitment, deter-
mination, and goals—why they are training in the dojo.
Facing the shinza, one can not help but notice the center-
piece. Two large *kanji* (Chinese ideograph) scrolls hang on
the walls, equally proportioned to the right and left of the
focal point. This focal point, a large wooden structure resembling an altar, dominates the expanse. Centered atop this
main section of the shrine rests a small photograph of

Kyokushin's founder, Mas Oyama. Flanking each side of the photograph are offerings. These are, in essence, offerings to the *kami* (spirit) of the shinza.

Shinza (shrine) at Honbu.

To outsiders unfamiliar with Asian and martial arts cultures and customs, the shinza may be mistaken as religious in nature. This is definitely not the case. The dojo shinza has nothing to do with religion. The dojo, a serious place of learning, houses a collection of individuals who share a common belief and purpose. This shared purpose or goal builds a strong bond between its members. This camaraderie dissolves egotism and individualism allowing all to focus as a group. This focus is the true mission of the dojo. When one becomes truly focused

The main dojo
(training hall)
of the honbu.

on the mission or the concept of and within the dojo, then a
strong spirit is produced. This spirit is felt and shared by each
member. Thus, energy and motivation can be gained from one
another during training. A true dojo will have a strong sense of
kami, or spirit, about it, and the shinza (shrine) exists to
remind us of that spirit and the purpose of the dojo.

Another noticeable fixture at the front of the main dojo, to the
left of the shinza, is the large *taiko* (drum). The taiko is hand-

made. The process of making one is painstaking, consisting of hollowing out a large portion of a log and shaping it into the proper contours and dimensions. Once the log is hollowed and contoured it is then sanded smooth and polished. The cured skins of animals are stretched across the openings at each end and fastened with ties. The drum can be sounded to signify the beginning and end to training. The taiko is also ceremonial in that when it is sounded, it calls upon the strong spirits of the dojo to enhance one's training.

The strong spirit within the main dojo of the Kyokushin honbu is apparent to all who have had the opportunity to train there. This spirit is manifested even more during the training sessions. Training within the dojo is physically taxing and mentally demanding. It requires extreme focus and concentration. Anything less and you will not finish. Strength to persevere, to continue, to push on through the demands of training can never diminish. The desire to succeed is etched on the faces of every student. Each and every student relies on the spirit emanating from each other in order to persevere. They also draw on the spirit of the hundreds of thousands of students who have gone before them and also on the spirit of the master, Oyama, himself. The spirit that is embodied in the dojo signifies the true essence of the warrior way as prescribed by the founder of Kyokushin karate. Mas Oyama followed the principles established by the samurai hundreds of years ago. That is why the karate of Oyama, Kyokushin, is today regarded as true *budo* karate.

For more than thirty years until his death, Oyama presided over his worldwide organization from this location. During his reign, Oyama built Kyokushin into the largest karate organization in the world, with a membership exceeding fifteen million in over one-hundred-and-twenty countries. He traveled extensively throughout the world promoting Kyokushin, personally instructing the various countries' branch chiefs and giving demonstrations to royalty, heads of state, as well as organizations including the FBI. His last trip to the United States was in 1992, when he attended The American International Karate Championships in Rochester, New York. Oyama authored several books on karate, including: *What is Karate?, This is Karate, Advanced Karate,* and *The Kyokushin Way.* Several films and videos have been made about Oyama—the man, his training, and his tournaments. In Japan, there was also a comic book series about him. Sosai Mas Oyama was recognized as the strongest karate man alive in his prime. He accomplished the feat of defeating three hundred top *karateka* in full-contact fighting that continued over two days. This record is unbroken and has never even been attempted by another.

It is said that throughout the years, a karate master makes up for any loss of strength with perfect timing and perception.

This theory definitely held true for Sosai Oyama, for even at the age of seventy he was virtually unbeatable. Until his death, Mas Oyama continued to instruct others in the techniques and philosophies of Kyokushin karate at his honbu.

The lives of Sosai and Mrs. Oyama revolved around the honbu. The honbu and Kyokushinkai *were* their lives. It is this dedication that allowed the honbu to become one of the most renowned karate training halls of all time. It is the responsibility of all Kyokushin students worldwide to ensure that the legacy of Sosai Oyama continues.

The author at Honbu

Author's students at Honbu

Author's wife (rt.), Honbu uchi-deshi and student.

Chapter 4

Oyama and Bushido

To Oyama, karate was everything. It was not a sport, but a discipline and a way of life. He believed that world peace could be achieved through the practice (including the philosophy) of karate. He felt so strongly about this that he came up with the idea of fighting a bull bare-handed, thinking that if he could defeat a bull with techniques of karate it would bring him worldwide recognition. This recognition, he thought, would give him a platform on which he could mount his world crusade for peace through the practice of karate.

The thought of world peace is really incomprehensible. To many, it is ludicrous, a pipe dream. There have been conflicts throughout the world since the beginning of time. Unrest continues at this very moment. Peace anytime in the near future, if ever, seems unlikely. So why such an undertaking by Oyama? We know from earlier chapters that Oyama was devastated after the war. He witnessed first-hand the ravages and

uncertainties that war leaves in its wake. He never wanted
others to be subject to such devastation again.

Oyama was an individual of strong principles and convictions. He was successful against all challenges. While others
would not even consider such challenges, Oyama accepted,
without thought of himself, and overcame them all. To
Oyama, world peace was but another challenge that others
shied away from. This "do or die" mentality of Oyama's is in
keeping with those of the *samurai* of feudal Japan. To serve,
as the samurai name implies, is exactly what the samurai
did—they served their lords. Samurai were of the warrior
class, soldiers so to speak, who lived by a code of conduct
with resolute characteristics. These characteristics set the
standard by which all samurai were to live in regards to man-
ners, ideals, and moral conscience.

This code of conduct was *bushido,* the "way of the warrior."
Samurai did not fear death or pain; they embraced it as a way
of life. In many instances the samurai paid with their lives for
their loyalty to their masters. This loyalty and dedication were
the essence of budo.

Bushido and budo were important concepts to Oyama.

Bushido can be compared to chivalry, with such noble qualities of courage, honor, and readiness to assist, which are also

characteristics of medieval knights. Both the knights and the samurai lived to protect their masters. Without hesitation, either would quickly lay down their own life in order to save the life of their master. What made the samurai more unique than the knights was that they would not only give their life to protect their master, but would actually *take* their own life if circumstances warranted. Any situation or circumstance in which the samurai failed or brought dis-

Mas Oyama in low fighting posture.

honor to his master constituted a grave misgiving, according to the code of bushido. Any such failure or disrespectful action could only be atoned for by the taking of one's own life. Many samurai, because of dishonor and/or failure, took their own lives via a ritual and method known as *seppuku*.

Seppuku allowed the condemned to redeem himself through
the absolute conviction by which the samurai lived: the giving
of his own life. Seppuku was not a simple attempt at suicide.
It had an order, a prescribed method that included witnesses
as well as a *haishaku* (second or aide) who was in most cases
a male friend. It was not a hurried attempt at self-murder. On
the contrary, seppuku was a meticulous practice, ceremonial
in itself, befitting the honor of bushido.

Although Oyama never did and never would have asked his
students to commit seppuku, he himself announced publicly,
in 1975, just prior to the First Kyokushin World Tournament,
that if the Japanese team lost he would commit seppuku.
Whether or not Oyama would have committed seppuku, one
will never know, for the Japanese team was victorious!

Oyama believed that anyone practicing the martial arts, in
particular karate, without adhering to the virtues of budo was
doing nothing more than engaging in a futile attempt at game-
playing. He believed in and emphasized the strong ideals of
budo, including but not limited to respect, self-discipline, perseverance, piety, and courtesy.

Looking at Mas Oyama's eleven mottoes, one can see his
strong devotion and convictions.

The martial way begins and ends with courtesy.
Therefore, be properly and genuinely courteous
at all times.

Following the martial way is like scaling a cliff—
continue upwards without rest. It demands absolute
and unfaltering devotion to the task at hand.

Strive to seize the initiative in all things, all the
time guarding against actions stemming from
selfish animosity or thoughtlessness.

Even for the martial artist, the place for money
cannot be ignored. Yet one should be careful never
to become attached to it.

The martial way is centered in posture.
Strive to maintain correct posture at all times.

The martial way begins with one thousand days
and is mastered after ten thousand days of training.

In the martial arts, introspection begets wisdom.
Always see contemplation on your actions as an
opportunity to improve.

The nature and purpose of the martial way is universal.
All selfish desires should be roasted in the tempering
fires of hard training.

The martial arts begin with a point and end with
a circle. Straight lines stem from this principle.

The true essence of the martial way can only
be realized through experience. Knowing this,
learn never to fear its demands.

Always remember: In the martial arts, the rewards
of a confident and grateful heart are truly abundant.

Oyama stunned and killed full-grown bulls with his empty-handed art, karate. He smashed stones, tiles, cement, wood, ice, and other materials with his bare hands. He fought and defeated three hundred consecutive karate fighters over the course of two days. He defeated professional boxers and wrestlers throughout the United States. He endured months upon months of solitude, high atop a mountain, perfecting his karate skills through rigorous training. Such training is not only unheard of today, but incomprehensible to most. It can only be compared to the demanding physical and mental training undertaken by today's elite special operations soldiers throughout the world. Though all of these undertakings required extreme physical prowess, Oyama was much more than brute strength.

Mas Oyama was a brilliant individual. He was a profound tactician and strategist. He extracted the best fighting techniques from various Chinese, Korean, and Japanese martial arts. He then encapsulated them into Kyokushin, a style that is still recognized today as among the most practical self-defense-oriented and strongest styles of karate.

Oyama never faltered in his quest to make Kyokushin karate the strongest. He maintained this desire until the day he died. He accomplished this by requiring his pupils to go beyond their limits, both mentally and physically. He asked and received 100 percent from his students. He could do this because he gave 110 percent of himself to them. He believed as an instructor, if one was not sweating twice as much as his students during training, then he was performing an injustice to them.

Kyokushin karate was able to become a worldwide organization, with a membership exceeding fifteen million, due to the instructors that Oyama produced—including such notables as Arneil, Barnes, Collins, Matsui, K. Midori, T. Nakamura, Nishida, S. Oyama, Y. Oyama, and Senpei. Although some have gone on to form their own highly respected and worthwhile organizations, their success is a testament to their mentor. The essence and basis of their training is and always will be that of Mas Oyama.

Oyama produced instructors to carry on his quest who were not only physically strong, but who also possessed a strong spirit. His own spirit was unshakable. The following is known as "The Kyokushin Spirit," as written by Oyama:

> *Keep one's head low (modest)*
> *eye's high (ambitious)*
> *reserved in speech (mind one's language)*
> *kind in heart (raise one's capacity).*
> *Serve other people with filial piety*
> *(serving one's parents good)*
> *as the starting point.*

Having the Kyokushin spirit, we must help each other to endeavor to make Kyokushin karate immortal.

This strong spirit still exists today in Kyokushin. Whether inside or outside the training hall, instructors are afforded the courtesy, by their students, of the positions they have earned. This is done by addressing the instructors and seniors with their respective titles of *sensei* or *shihan*. Respect and courtesy between teachers and students is paramount. Without the aforementioned addressing of one's seniors, then what we have is karate without budo. We will then succumb to nothing more than a sport or game of tag, as so many other so-called styles have done. This will never happen to Kyokushin.

Oyama lived his own life with the same portion of self-discipline as that of the ancient samurai. He did not fear death; he could not. To fear death would not have allowed him to undertake the challenges that he faced. Without self-denial and sacrifices, Oyama would not have been triumphant in his zeal to promote the merits of karate.

Oyama's strong conviction of self-denial is clearly evident in the third line of Kyokushin's dojo *kun* (training hall oath). The dojo kun of Kyokushinkai is a modification of the original training hall oath written by Isshinryu founder Tatsuo Shimabuku. The dojo kun is recited aloud by every student at each training session. The third line reads:

> *"With true vigor we will seek to cultivate a spirit of self-denial."*

According to Oyama, if people are willing to make sacrifices and acquire self-denial, they will be successful in all their endeavors.

Bushido, "the way of the warrior," embodies the concept of self-denial. Life, as viewed by those following the way of bushido, is meaningless if one is not totally dedicated to one's master. Money and material items are insignificant. What is important to those living the code of bushido is total commitment and dedication. Total commitment for the samurai included giving one's life in the defense of the master if necessary.

It was this total commitment and self-denial that was so profound to Oyama. Out of this same honor and respect, Oyama reasoned, why could one not maintain this same conviction to karate? Oyama believed he could. Oyama dedicated his life to karate. This was not without sacrifices. In the words of Oyama:

"Without budo, there is no karate."

Chapter 5

Kyokushin—
The Ultimate Truth

The ultimate truth. What is it? Thought provoking as it is, the responses received from students over the years range from the sublime to looks of bewilderment, as if they were asked to describe the theory of relativity. Oyama believed that truth resides within each of us, and only careful introspection allows for the understanding and acceptance of such truth. When asked to define the ultimate truth, people have given the following answers:

- Understanding the difference between good and evil.
- Knowing when to accept criticism.
- Honoring thy father and mother.
- Knowing that God does or does not exist.
- At death, learning all the mysteries of life.

But the most common response of all is simply nothing, because for many there is simply no comprehension of even the question itself.

I wonder if it is that they really do not know or that they do not want to know? But then why would anyone want to know the ultimate truth? Perhaps it is something better left alone, for the answer may require thinking, acting, responding. In this day of "political correctness," perhaps the best response is to say nothing at all. At least then you avoid the risk of offending a thin-skinned individual or society. Then perhaps there are worse reasons for not wanting to know, like changing preconceived beliefs.

Many individuals do things a certain way because that is how they were instructed. Their parents did it this way and their parents before them. Therefore, it must be done the same way. If something has survived being handed down from generation to generation then it must be the correct way and/or the truth. Why change it? Why question it?

Because it is necessary.

Society needs individualism. For the most part, however, society stifles this very phenomenon. Why look for an easier or better way to accomplish something, when doing so may require change? And to change is unthinkable for many. To change requires facing the unknown. And everyone knows that fear of the unknown is paramount and stressful.

Mas Oyama believed that in order to seek the truth, one must be able to set themselves free from material possessions. In addition, he believed one must set themselves free in their thinking. One way to do this was through Kyokushin karate training. Karate requires that we train the mind, body, and spirit as one. Today, for the most part, because of ignorance or the nonexistence of budo within karate, there is no unity of mind, body, and spirit.

Karate, in general, has become a sport, a game of tag. The emphasis is on the material aspect rather than the development of the student. Weekend after weekend in cities all across the country tournaments promoted as karate are being held. Hundreds of individuals of all ages, from all walks of life, can be seen in various designs, colors, and patterns of the training uniform. All with the same purpose in mind: to leave with the biggest trophy in hand. The real meaning behind "winning or losing" escapes them. For they have not been taught that the competition is a personal test of the self. They have not been exposed to the premise that one learns from losing. There is no thought of defeat. This is clearly evident after witnessing such a student lose a match. The student may argue with the judges or even, as I have seen, challenge the judge to "step outside." They may argue with their instructor or place the blame for their losing on the instructor. They may refuse to shake hands with their opponent and storm from the ring mouthing obscenities. I have even seen a child berate a parent. Too much emphasis is placed on taking a trophy back to the school where an ego-starved instructor can display it with the countless others that cram the windows or any other unoccupied space within. This is a true lack of respect, and respect is a virtue of budo.

The Japanese have a saying, *"Nana korobi ya oki,"* which means that in learning if you fall down seven times, you get up eight times. In other words, if you fail, keep on trying until you succeed and never give up. It also means that if you get knocked down you should learn something from it, such as what was the cause of your being knocked down. Learn what was the true cause and avoid it in order not to be knocked down again.

Such sayings as this can be expounded upon, and instructors should incorporate lecture time into training to introduce these thoughts to students. The student can then contemplate these thoughts during the time set aside in the dojo for meditation. Such thoughts should become aides from which the student can learn. They should be applied not only to their karate training, but to life in general. Unfortunately, such sayings, lectures, and meditations are not practiced in most karate schools—perhaps a reason why such negative actions and behaviors are portrayed at tournaments.

The purpose of Kyokushin karate training is not just to learn self-defense. It is not just to get stronger physically. It is not to see who can punch or kick the hardest. It is not to see which student does the best kata. It is not to produce full-contact, knockdown fighters. Kyokushin karate training is intended to make each student better. By this, I mean each time a student leaves the dojo after a training session, they should be better than when they entered: better physically, mentally, and spiritually. This is to say that they should not only become well-rounded karate practitioners, but well-rounded individuals through and through. The discipline, hard work, concentration, and respect demonstrated in the dojo is the student's true being. Applying these same traits to one's daily life is the purpose of Kyokushin karate training.

Kokoro means mind, body, spirit, or inner being. Kyokushin karate trains the mind, body, and spirit. Again, this is why Kyokushin is a true budo karate—it polishes rough edges in its practitioners.

Mas Oyama, motivational speakers, teachers, and others of their kind believe that individuals can change. The question is, do they want to change? Once again, it is the change, the uncertainty, the fear of the unknown, the comfort of routine that prevents many from discovering their potential and establishing their true selves.

To see who we really are requires introspection. Until a sincere introspection is taken, one will continue to live with the doubts, the fear, the uncertainties, the lack of self-confidence, the abuse. A sincere introspection involves a close scrutiny of one's character and constitution. For the most part, this scrutiny will produce the possibility one will encounter something they do not like, can not accept about themselves, the truth, and so on.

The ultimate truth comes from deep within. We must look deep within ourselves, underneath the surface of the self in order to understand. We need to ask ourselves, "What purpose do we serve to mankind?" To achieve the ultimate truth, one must be willing to liberate oneself from personal oppressions. Mas Oyama was a firm believer in this concept. This is why the name Kyokushin is so appropriate to his own thoughts, deeds, and actions. This is why he chose the name Kyokushin for his style of karate. Kyokushin means "the ultimate truth."

Mas Oyama's Kyokushin karate is recognized throughout the martial arts world as *"the strongest karate"* because of its intense, demanding physical regiments, unbeaten fighting records, Oyama's life-threatening battles with bulls, his spectacular feats of breaking, the non-stop 100-man fights accomplished by his students, and a worldwide membership exceeding fifteen million. These are the physical accomplishments of Kyokushin. But these accomplishments alone are not what has allowed Kyokushin karate to endure the sands of time, to continue to be recognized as *the strongest karate."*

It is also what has come from within Mas Oyama, what he thought and inspired his students to accomplish, and those accomplishments of every student who persevered and along the way succeeded in the strongest style of karate: Kyokushin—the ultimate truth.

Chapter 6

Osu

O *su!* . . . *Osu!* . . . The utterance of the word *osu* is endless within the Kyokushin organization. It is heard over and over again through training sessions in the dojo. Fellow Kyokushin students address one another with either a handshake or bow and the simultaneous pronouncement of "osu."

Osu is a word of many interpretations and purposes. It can be a response, such as, "Yes, I understand," when the instructor gives a command or demonstrates a technique. It is also an acknowledgment to the training hall and its occupants upon entering. It is also the respect and gratitude paid to the instructor, seniors, and the training hall after finishing a training session. When the instructor calls out to the student to perform a kata or demonstrate a technique, osu becomes the response, "Yes, I am ready."

The expression of the word osu eventually becomes so involuntary that often, and sometimes without realizing it, many students use it in public settings. For example, your academic teacher asks you a question and you respond with "osu." A supervisor praises your job performance and instead of replying with "thank you," osu leaps from your mouth.

Unfortunately, saying osu becomes so involuntary that we take it for granted. To many students it is something we say because seniors told us to do so or because we have heard everyone else say it. Osu becomes just another part of training, the same as a kiai. Many individuals say it but do not understand the true essence of osu.

So, then, why do we use osu and what does it really mean?

Osu is derived from the Japanese term *oshi shinobu*. The first word *oshi* means to maintain, to keep up. *Shinobu* means to bear, to endure. In Kyokushin and other martial arts, the contraction "osu" means to persevere, persist, keep going, be patient. In essence, osu means to be patient in your training and never give up. Every time the word osu is said or heard, it should suggest to us the need to be diligent. If we are diligent in our training, the benefits we derive from Kyokushin will far outweigh the sweat and discomfort.

All adults must face the pressures of life. Parents have the responsibility and stress to see that their children have the proper upbringing. They must contend with the expenses of education, medical coverage, clothing, and nourishment; music lessons, prom dresses, drivers licenses; and so on. There are mortgage payments, insurance payments, and auto repairs. Worries about job security, illness, maintaining a spousal relationship—the list is endless. Young people also are not immune when it comes to the pressures of life. Advancing in school, friendships, social status, the opposite gender, society's temptations, are but a few of the dilemmas young people face. Life is full of peaks and valleys that everyone must face. Similar peaks and valleys exist in one's training. How one chooses to face them is what often makes the difference between success and failure.

Some individuals dwell on the peaks, some on the valleys. Those who live in the valleys and dwell on their discomforts are always feeling sorry for themselves. They constantly think *"woe is me."* They allow every little muscle ache and sniffle to prohibit them from coming to work, fulfilling their obligations, or getting to the dojo. Others allow their spouse or partner to dictate control. Many individuals live above their means. Then there are those individuals who allow a clock and calendar to control their lives. People who fit into these categories are never happy or satisfied. They are disgruntled with their employer and job. They seem to always be suffering from some illness or ailment. When they speak of their spouse or partner, which is seldom, they do so negatively. The people who fall into the above categories allow other things and other people to control them, rather than having the authority over their lives. They have negative attitudes and often fail at whatever they attempt. They are opposite from those who focus on the peaks, the doers of the world.

"Doers" project a demeanor of confidence, authority, and satisfaction. The reason for this positive attitude is because they are in charge of their lives. They may not always be totally happy or satisfied with their lives, but they do not allow unhappiness to detract from their obligations. They set their sights on advancement and they are always looking to improve themselves and their future. These individuals are rarely absent from work or the dojo. They understand that reducing or eliminating stress is essential for well-being. They speak often of their spouse and of their shared activities. You seldom see one without the other, as they are happy and sound in their relationship. These individuals live within their means. They usually do not flaunt material possessions or need status symbols. They make time to accomplish goals. These individuals have positive attitudes and are usually successful in their endeavors.

Both categories of individuals can be seen training in any given dojo. What sets them apart from each other in the dojo is the same thing that sets them apart outside the dojo: *their attitude*. Each category has a significantly different approach to training. Those with the positive outlook on life (doers), have a higher attendance record. Doers keep unpleasant experiences of the day to themselves. Doers do not compete with other students, show off, or have big egos. Doers are more confident in their performance and advance at a faster rate. Each individual has his own reasons for attending the dojo and regardless of the category they fall into they can still derive positive benefits. They only need to open their eyes and minds to the comprehensive opportunities that their training offers. Then they must practice the essence of osu— being patient and never giving up.

The most difficult aspect of Kyokushin karate is getting to class. Excuses for not attending class are easy to invent and they are endless. A bad day at work or school, the dog interrupted my sleep, I am sore from training last week, the price of gas rose again. These excuses sound foolish because they are. There are no excuses, except if you want to fail. Instead of wasting energy inventing excuses one should redirect that energy into their training.

Training at the dojo, especially after a difficult day at work or home, can be the most rewarding of accomplishments. By not allowing the outside pressures to take over and win, students can take control over their lives. The reward or benefit is the

victorious feeling one derives from overcoming adversity. As
the students realize this, they inject that positive feeling and
energy into their training. On days like this, a student will
experience some of their very best training. This is because
the student *persevered*.

Upon entering the dojo, the student immediately says "Osu."
This osu is an acknowledgment to the dojo and to all who
train there. It should also be a reminder to the student to be
patient *with themselves and fellow students*. Osu should also
remind students to abandon the pressures of the day. All students have bad days. Unleashing one's troubles in the dojo
and on fellow classmates hinders everyone's performance.
Osu also reminds us to be strong.

Every time we hear osu throughout the training session, it
should motivate us. But it should also remind us that what
transpires during training in the dojo is a world apart from our
day-to-day activities outside the dojo. For example, the *dogi*
is unlike anything in one's wardrobe. To assume the kneeling
posture of *seiza* is uncomfortable, even to Asians. Countless
repetitions of basic techniques and kata tax physical and
mental reserves. To *kiai*—shout at the top of one's voice—is
unacceptable anywhere else. These are just some of the experiences that bind students in the dojo. The camaraderie and
positive energy shared among fellow karateka is something
only a few experience. There is a unique feeling that comes

from knowing every student shares the vigorous physical and mental undertaking of the dojo. These unique feelings manifest in everyone when training comes to a close and students realize that perseverance made them stronger, both as individuals and as a collective entity of the dojo.

Without a doubt, there is a bond between the students in the dojo. This bond exists because of many reasons. All students share and commit to the same goal. Side by side, students push to their physical limitations. The sweat a student sheds during class belongs to every member of the dojo. During a promotion examination, palms become wet, bodies tense. Everyone encourages those testing with shouts and gestures of encouragement. No one wants to see anyone fail. An exhilaration of joy is felt by all at the conclusion of the test.

During training, the intensity level is high. As kiai resound throughout the dojo, energy transpires from student to student. This energy fuels the drive for everyone to push on. Junior students observe their seniors. The seniors' performances motivate others. The instructor executes techniques, counting out the repetitions. He is sweating twice as hard as anyone else. During kumite, anxieties are high. Again, students cheer on each other. When fighting is over, another feeling of exhilaration and accomplishment comes over everyone.

The aim of karate training is to become a better person. Through karate training, one learns to overcome adversities put upon them in the dojo. By conquering these adversities, a student gains confidence. This confidence carries over into all other aspects of their lives. Students with a positive outlook on life, the *doers,* become even stronger. Students of the negative outlook, those who reason through excuses, realize they are the ones who control their destiny. In time, their negative views diminish and a positive attitude emerges. Through perseverance, each time a student leaves the dojo he is a better person. This is the purpose of karate and of the dojo. This is the true spirit of osu.

Chapter 7

Training

"One becomes a beginner after one thousand days of training and an expert after ten thousand days of practice."

—Mas Oyama

Mas Oyama's beliefs in the virtues, ideals, and practicality of the martial arts were so strong that he devoted his life to the art of karate. Oyama began training in the martial arts at the age of nine. His practice at this time was in Chinese kempo. The initial techniques of kempo were known as *shakuriki* (eighteen techniques). The eighteen techniques Oyama studied were under the tutelage of Mr. Yi, who was an employee on the farm owned by Oyama's sister. A few years later, Oyama began practicing Shotokan karate under Gichin Funakoshi. By the age of fifteen, Oyama was a shodan and by the age of eighteen he had earned his nidan. Oyama also trained and earned his black belt in judo.

Still not satisfied with his martial arts knowledge, Oyama sought out other instructors. He wanted to learn all he could about the martial arts in general, karate in particular. More eager than ever to train, Oyama found a karate instructor named Nei-Chu So, a practitioner of the Gojo-ryu style of karate. Oyama trained diligently under the auspices of So, and by the age of twenty-three earned a *yondan* (fourth level black belt). It was also at the age of twenty-three that Oyama's life would take a drastic shift away from his current ideology.

As the story goes, Oyama was twenty-three years of age and WWII had just ended. Because of his size and martial arts skills, Oyama was employed as a bouncer, bodyguard, and all-around safeguard by less-than-desirable members of society. One evening he became embroiled in an argument while working. During the argument the antagonist provoked Oyama, who retaliated by striking the individual. Oyama was arrested, found guilty of the offense, and imprisoned for six months. It was during this imprisonment that Oyama, reflecting on himself and the violence of his employment, vowed that when he was released he would devote his life to karate and its philosophies.

After his release from jail, Oyama sought the guidance once more of his karate instructor, Nei-Chu So. So was a demanding instructor, as well as a strict disciplinarian. He chastised Oyama in a manner that a father may do a son. He condemned Oyama's attitude, associates, and recent mode of employment. So went on to tell Oyama that if he continued with his current lifestyle, he would end up in trouble once more. Oyama was reminded of his size, strength, and karate abilities. So berated Oyama for letting his talents and life go to waste, imploring Oyama to change his unfavorable disposition and manner. Oyama asked So how he should go about the difficult task of changing. So's reply was that Oyama should impart his knowledge of karate to others.

So's recommendation required a thorough test before Oyama would be permitted to teach. The test proposed by So was for Oyama to isolate himself for the purpose of training. Only after concluding such a commitment could one understand the true meaning of karate, So advised. Oyama respected the insights of his instructor and pledged to Nei-Chu So that he would do as his teacher suggested. He would isolate himself and train like no one had done before. Oyama had already pledged to himself during his incarceration that he would devote his life to karate. He just wanted assurance from his teacher that he was worthy of such an objective.

The beginning of this devotion began in 1946, when Oyama, equipped with only reading material and provisions to sustain life, set out for Mt. Minobu, in Chiba prefecture. Mt. Minobu is a remote area regarded as a place of enlightenment for another famous martial artist. It is here, in the same spot selected by Oyama, that Miyamoto Musashi developed his Nito-ryu system of sword fighting. Musashi is regarded as the greatest swordsman in Japanese history. Oyama selected Mt. Minobu because of the association Musashi had with the area. What better place to immerse oneself in training, thought Oyama. If this area proved so beneficial to Musashi, then perhaps it would do the same for Oyama.

Oyama and one of his students, Yashiro, set out with the intention of spending three years on Mt. Minobu. Together they set up a make-shift structure that would protect them from the elements. Oyama had a benefactor back in Tokyo who agreed to furnish Oyama with the necessary staples to sustain him and Yashiro for the three years of training. Here, in total isolation, they would train diligently for the next three years in what they knew best: karate.

One evening, only six months into their mountain training, Yashiro, under the cover of darkness, abandoned Oyama. Oyama would later relate that he did not hold any ill feelings towards Yashiro, because the loneliness Yashiro felt was unbearable. Social contact is what Yashiro missed and needed, and Oyama could not be upset with him for only wanting what was natural.

Oyama, now alone, continued to train. On more than one occasion Oyama also felt the loneliness tugging at his emotions. There were several times when the thought of quitting and leaving the mountain entered his mind. When he encountered those thoughts of quitting, Oyama would counter them by training harder. Through his training he was able to withstand the pressures of loneliness and endure his mission. After the eighteenth month of training, circumstances prohibited Oyama's benefactor from continuing his support. Once again, Oyama was devastated. Oyama pondered his situation, but could think of no way to continue his training. Without the proper necessities he would be unable to sustain such a rigorous venture. Perhaps this setback was fate, he thought, letting him know it was the right time to bring his karate to the attention of the world. He reflected on the last eighteen months. The solitude was unmerciful, but he had endured and not given in. It was time to leave the mountains.

Oyama's eighteen months of training was truly nothing short of masochistic. He subjected himself to a training regimen that began at dawn and continued until dusk. On many occasions his training lasted well into the darkness of night. There were occasional breaks from the physical training to replenish his body with food and to re-energize his mind through meditation and reading. The long days of training surely depleted Oyama both physically and mentally. In addition, the isolation took its toll on him. Loneliness, Oyama discovered, is a worthy adversary. However, he remained focused, as he was becoming *one with karate.*

Oyama pushed beyond the limits of human endurance throughout his training. In the early morning hours he would rise from his sleep, eat, and then begin training. The morning session usually consisted of performing kihon (basic techniques such as blocks, strikes, thrusts, and kicks) hundreds of times over. This was followed by kata, a formal exercise consisting of a series of prearranged movements designed with self-defense applications.

When practicing a kata, the individual begins in a pre-determined spot. From there the moves are pre-directed in various angles as the individual executes blocks, strikes, kicks, and counters against an imaginary opponent or opponents. The completed kata ends in the same position and place where it began. The kata of lower-level ranks contain approximately twenty moves each. Kata of the mid- and high-level ranks may include movements that exceed fifty counts. Oyama would practice each kata one hundred times in succession daily.

His training methods were simple—some would even say crude—and they were demanding. The surroundings of the mountain and settings became Oyama's training hall. He used boulders and fallen trees for weight and resistance training. Running up and down the steep mountain slopes developed his cardiovascular endurance and leg strength. Leaping over plants and bushes contributed to his agility and jumping abilities. He conditioned his mind and body through meditation under the battering of icy waterfalls. Using trees as makiwara (striking posts), Oyama struck the trees thousands of times over, enough to kill them. This unorthodox makiwara training tempered his bare hands, arms, and legs into effective instruments of power and destruction. This manner of training was a daily ritual followed by Oyama for eighteen consecutive months. Pitting oneself against nature and its elements was to Oyama a true test of one's dedication and perseverance.

Oyama's desire to succeed was fueled by a passage from a book that Oyama had read as a young teen. However, his understanding of the book was not realized until he read it again during his six-month incarceration. The book was "Musashi," by Eiji Yoshikawa. It recounted the life and times of Miyamoto Musashi, regarded as the greatest swordsman in Japanese history. In one passage, Musashi is admonished by one of his elders, Takuan Soho. Soho tells the young Musashi to use the strength and knowledge he has for the sake of other people, if not for the sake of the whole nation. He goes on to say that Musashi should be ashamed of having been born a human being but in so far failing to live like one. He continues to admonish Musashi for behaving like a wild animal. Soho finishes by telling Musashi that if he continues in such a manner, he will end up in a disgraceful way. After reading this passage, Oyama saw himself as Soho saw Musashi, following the wrong path. It is said that there and

then, at the moment of this reading, Oyama pledged to make
karate and the essence of karate his life.

Oyama's pledge to devote his life to karate went beyond himself at the moment of that decision. Being a patriot, Oyama
was devastated by what he witnessed in the aftermath of the
war in Japan. He, like many others at the close of the war,
wanted world peace. He thought, what better vehicle to bring
people together for peace than what he already knew and had
at his disposal, his karate-do—"way of karate."

World peace? Oyama wondered if he was crazy or mad. He
knew many men greater than he had tried and failed. Oyama
must have asked himself why he thought he could change
things. Whether or not he thought he could make a difference, he persevered with his ideals.

Oyama was convinced that his success in such an undertaking depended on his karate. His eighteen months in the
mountains took him to a point in his training where his physical, mental, and spiritual dimensions were starting to come
together. But there was still more training and work to be
done before he could accept karate as the instrument he
thought it could be. Oyama understood there could be no
doubts about the effectiveness of his karate. If he doubted
any part of his karate in the least, then others would also
doubt. Oyama was determined to prove to himself and to the

world that karate was not only effective for self-defense, but applicable for achieving well-being. He also understood that the only way to be sure of this was to test himself and karate under the most extreme conditions, even if it meant mental anguish and physical pain for himself. Oyama pushed himself harder until the time came to leave the mountains and show the world *his* karate.

But how was this to be accomplished?

A short time after returning from the mountains, the first karate tournament since the end of the war was held in Japan. Oyama entered the tournament hoping if he was victorious it would aid in his display of karate to the world. Oyama was undefeated and was crowned Grand Champion of the tournament. However, he was disillusioned with the karate he witnessed at the tournament and felt that something was missing. Disillusioned and still not satisfied with his own abilities, Oyama set out for the mountains once again. This time Oyama selected Mt. Kiyozumi, again in Chiba prefecture, as his training site.

As before, Oyama carried out the harsh training and isolation he had come to know. Many of Oyama's training sessions exceeded fourteen hours. In order to maintain such a demanding schedule, Oyama included the practice of Zen meditation. These meditation sessions were conducted outdoors, at various times throughout the day and evening. As it had come to be with his karate training, inclement weather did not stop his meditation sessions. Wind, rain, and cold became tools that enhanced his meditation. Striving to train even harder, he needed to abandon all thoughts of hardships and difficulties. To accomplish this task, Oyama began meditating under icy waterfalls. He would relate later that this form of meditation was the only way to cleanse his mind of negative thoughts. Oyama would continue his isolated training for one year before returning again to society.

Many of Oyama's associates criticized and scorned him for his training methods and were suspect of his motives. Oyama took these reactions in stride. He had given two and a half hard years of his life in the pursuit of perfecting his karate. He would not let it be in vain. He believed in his heart that his aspirations were meaningful. He challenged himself to come up with a way to show the world the capacity of karate. What better way, he thought, than to challenge himself again, but this time in front of the world. It was at this moment that Oyama came up with the idea of empty-handedly battling a bull.

And so it came to be, Oyama traveled the world, successfully fighting bulls. His recognition grew as he was invited by countries throughout the world to demonstrate his karate. Although Oyama did not bring about world peace through karate, he never stopped trying. He did show that it was possible to bring together people from various nations. Whether it was at his Kyokushin *honbu* (headquarters) in Ikebukuro, his World Tournament in Tokyo, or the hundreds of other tournaments and seminars he conducted worldwide, he brought people together from all nationalities and all walks of life. These people, in the spirit of karate, found peace and harmony through the omnipotence of Kyokushin karate and one man—Mas Oyama.

It is ironic that Oyama and the author of the book *Musashi,* the same book that Oyama credits with changing his life, would cross paths. When Oyama founded Kyokushin, he called upon the author, Eiji Yoshikawa, for his assistance. Oyama and Yoshikawa collaborated in writing the *dojo kun* (training hall oath) for the Kyokushin organization. Just as Musashi is recognized as the greatest swordsman in Japanese history, Oyama is recognized by many in the martial arts world as the greatest karateka (karate practitioner) of his time.

Oyama's accomplishments in building the world's largest karate organization, *tameshiwari,* undefeated fighting records, and battling bulls are untouched even today. His extreme personal training methods have never even been attempted by any other karate person.

When asked about training and to what a person should devote his time, Oyama replied:

"Training. Train more than you sleep. No matter what course you pursue, you will have no regrets if you make this a hard-and-fast rule. Human beings are the only creatures on earth that are conscious of what being alive means—the highest premium is placed on acquired abilities. Humans are capable of virtually limitless degradation; they are also capable of virtually limitless improvement and achievement. Success depends on goals and the diligence in pursuing them. Such a person will never waste a moment of their time."

Three training sessions per week is the average attendance of most students. Based on this number of classes attended, the quote at the beginning of this chapter equates to the following: one thousand days at three days per week is 6.4 years. Ten thousand days at three days per week is 64.1 years. This truly portrays the notion that training is never really over.

Chapter 8

Young Lions of Oyama

Every year at the Kyokushin headquarters in the Ikebukuro district of Tokyo, a special graduation ceremony is held. This ceremony recognizes those young men, who for the last three years devoted every waking moment of their lives to the practice of Kyokushin karate. For them this three-year ordeal was for the honor and purpose of becoming Kyokushin karate instructors. These devout students are known as "The Young Lions of Oyama." What sets these students apart from all the other Kyokushin students is that they are *uchi-deshi*—live-in students.

The uchi-deshi program is three consecutive years in duration. The uchi-deshi and their curriculum were overseen by Mas Oyama personally. Each year, several young men, both Japanese and foreign, would apply for enrollment into the uchi-deschi program at the honbu, under the guidance of Oyama. Of the hundred or so who apply each year, less than twenty are accepted. Acceptance as an uchi-deshi was determined by Oyama, who would personally interview every candidate. During the interview Oyama would carefully scrutinize each candidate, as he was looking for individuals who displayed the willingness and desire to succeed. Of those individuals fortunate enough to have been selected, only two or three would graduate. For many of them, the next three years would be the most intense undertaking of their lives.

Regular Kyokushin karate training is intense and physical, and students are scrutinized very closely for mistakes or the formation of bad habits throughout a training session. Uchi-deshi students are scrutinized even more so for mistakes, bad habits, and laziness. This scrutiny makes their training even more intense than that of regular students. For the uchi-deshi, it is like being under a microscope. The added pressure of the scrutiny can be unbearable and not all make it through. For three years, these students' lives are filled with nothing but training and the philosophies of Kyokushin karate. In addition, their curriculum includes the following: first-aid, weight-resistance (strength) training, cardiovascular enhancement (running), motivational techniques, leadership, instructor techniques, Zen readings, and meditation. The uchi-deshi program is so demanding that it consumes all of their waking time. Their adherence to this schedule creates a lifestyle that would seem abnormal to outsiders.

Located behind the Kyokushin headquarters in Tokyo is a structure known to its occupants and Kyokushin students as *Wakajish-ryo*, meaning "Young Lion's Dormitory." It is where the uchi-deshi from the Kyokushin honbu reside. Because the program is three years long, the uchi-deshi are divided into three groups for the first, second, and third years. The first-year group is the largest with each group becoming smaller as attrition takes its toll. Obviously the third-year group is the smallest. In some years there have only been one or two uchi-deshi remaining in the third-year group. There is a hierarchy in the dormitory as well as in their training sessions. Three-year students oversee second-year students, including disciplinary measures and setting orders for chores in and out of the dormitory and training hall. Second-year students in turn oversee first-year students.

The *sempai/kohai* (senior/junior) relationship is very much in existence within the uchi-deshi program. The uchi-deshi have little if any contact with outsiders, and only when they grocery shop for the dormitory or when visiting students train at the honbu. Uchi-deshi were also called upon to run errands for Mas Oyama and honbu instructors, as well as being Oyama's drivers. To the uchi-deshi, serving their seniors, in particular Oyama, was a privilege and an honor. The uchi-deshi lifestyle is far removed from the outside world and the world today in general. Because the program taxes the physical, mental, and emotional limits of each uchi-deshi, Oyama had great compassion for them. The training they receive for the three years is the best the Kyokushin organization has to offer.

The uchi-deshi schedule begins with a 6:00 A.M. class. For the next two hours they train outdoors on their physical strength and endurance. The session begins with a warm-up for the muscles and joints. This is followed by a four-to-six-mile run. The run can take a different course each morning and may also vary in conditions. One day the run may include several fast sprints mixed with the normal pace. Other days it may include running up and down several stairs found throughout the course. Or it may include sprints, stairs, and the normal pace. The run is often immediately followed by several hundred repetitions of various kicks and strikes and then two hundred push-ups and two hundred squats. The uchi-deshi then run back to the honbu where they work on kumite (fighting) drills. To close out the two-hour session, the uchi-deshi perform two to three hundred sit-ups and then a cool down that includes various stretching routines. All this is done before they go to breakfast.

Breakfast for the uchi-deshi, while Sosai was alive, was a time honored tradition. This was because Oyama would eat breakfast with the uchi-deshi. However, I am sure there were times when the uchi-deshi secretly wished he would not. Whenever

one ate with Sosai Oyama, food was not wasted. He made
sure that whatever you put on your plate you finished. This
was because during the war food was at a premium and
many food items were rationed. Oyama grew to appreciate
many of the things that are taken for granted in life, especially
food. On many occasions one would see Oyama serving the
food. This was his way of making sure everyone ate enough
to sustain their training. Oyama himself was a big eater but
he was also a very big man. Many uchi-deshi and others present at a meal with Oyama were so stuffed that it made training afterwards difficult.

Two days each week Oyama personally conducted the two-
hour uchi-deshi classes. On other days the uchi-deshi
classes, also two hours in duration, were conducted by various other honbu instructors. These classes were only
attended by uchi-deshi. For regular students, kayo-no-deshi
(walk-in students), there are four two-hour classes daily. It is
mandatory for all uchi-deshi to attend all of these classes.
Each uchi-deshi is permitted two hours each day for personal
training. Here the lone uchi-deshi trains in whatever he
wants. This may be kihon, kata, ido-geiko (moving training),
or renraku (transition). If an uchi-deshi is having difficulty
with a particular technique or kata in the regular classes, he
is encouraged to train in this area during his personal session.

The Young Lions program is designed to develop students into future Kyokushin instructors. Because of this, they undergo all facets of Kyokushin requirements, including basic technique training, philosophy, physical conditioning, first-aid, and instructor techniques.

They must learn how to instruct others, while being instructed themselves. Three-year uchi-deshi students are called upon to instruct at some of the classes for the walk-in students. They may also be called upon to instruct when foreign members visit honbu. And because of the students' close personal relationships with Oyama, it was understood that their performance in the dojo and honbu was of a higher standard than the walk-in students.

Uchi-deshi are very noticeable from the moment one enters the honbu. There is one, if not two uchi-deshi "at the ready" at the front door at all times. Their duties while at this station are many. They open the door and greet students, visiting instructors, and seniors. If the individual who arrives at the door is a senior instructor, they will greet him and ask if there is anything he needs. At times the uchi-deshi may be instructed by the senior to bring items in from the senior's vehicle. If it is raining, it is not uncommon to see the uchi-deshi go outside and escort the senior with an umbrella. Another purpose of the uchi-deshi presence at the door of the honbu dates back to earlier times when it was necessary to ward-off possible altercations with students from other karate styles.

In these early days when Oyama was building his Kyokushin enrollment, many students from other styles of karate in Japan sought out his instruction. Most of these students did so without the knowledge or permission of their other instructor. As time passed it became evident to these instructors that their students were training elsewhere. This was evident as these students were becoming much more powerful in their fighting skills. There are many stories of these students from the other schools who were training with Oyama, returning to their schools and inflicting injuries on the other students. These injuries were during kumite training. Some might wonder why students would juggle between Oyama and their own instructor rather than just quitting the latter. It was not that the instruction they were receiving from their own instructor was poor. It was that they were seeking out instruction that would enhance their skills. This was especially true in the style of *jissen-kumite* (full-contact fighting without pads) embraced by Oyama and his Kyokushin style.

When these other instructors learned of their students' association with Oyama, many became enraged. Several of these instructors sent groups of their students to the Kyokushin honbu threatening and challenging Oyama and his students. The uchi-deshi became the first line of defense against such actions. Lined up side-by-side outside the Kyokushin honbu doors, the uchi-deshi stood ready to defend Oyama and the Kyokushinkai. If a situation occurred requiring the assistance of the uchi-deshi, an alarm, located behind the uchi-deshi dormitory, would sound day or night to call the uchi-deshi, who would run to the front of the honbu and take their positions of defense against outside rivals. The hierarchy within the uchi-deshi structure prevails in these situations as it is the responsibility of the least senior uchi-deshi to first intervene if a confrontation is inevitable. It is his duty and honor to defend his seniors and dojo. The other uchi-deshi would intervene and assist if necessary in the order from least senior to the highest. This is another example of the sempai/kohai relationship. This tradition of standing guard at the honbu doors to defend Kyokushinkai, if it becomes necessary, is maintained today by the uchi-deshi. Another tradition maintained by the uchi-deshi is their consistent promotion of Kyokushin karate.

Maintaining the integrity and legacy of Kyokushinkai is the mission of those who graduate from the uchi-deshi program. The uchi-deshi carry out this mission through various avenues of exposure that promote Kyokushin karate. These avenues include participation in karate tournaments, demonstrations for the general public, and instruction in the art. The uchi-deshi are able to accomplish this as a result of their thorough training. To say the training received by the uchi-deshi is comprehensive is an understatement. It was the hope of Oyama and the honbu instructors that these students would carry on the Kyokushin instruction in Japan and around the world.

The uchi-deshi of today are still meant to be instructors for Kyokushinkai and diplomats of Kyokushin karate. As diplomats, one of their duties is to represent Kyokushin in the various karate tournaments throughout Japan each year. The format for the tournaments in which the uchi-deshi partake is jissen-kumite. Jissen-kumite is a free-fighting, knockdown style, without the use of protective equipment. The uchi-deshi do not partake in these tournaments until after the end of their first year of training, since participants at the knockdown tournaments must be of the black-belt rank. Most of the other contestants in the tournaments have been black belts for several years.

Usually it takes several years for most students to attain the rank of black belt in Kyokushin karate. The advancement in the uchi-deshi program is first level black belt at the end of the first year. This rank is known as shodan—beginner level. This advancement continues for each additional year within the uchi-deshi program. Nidan—second level—at the end of two years, and sandan—third level—at the end of the three-year program. After completion of the three-year program, uchi-deshi are ready to establish their own dojos throughout the world. In their various dojos the uchi-deshi will carry on the traditions of Kyokushinkai by instructing others as certified instructors of Kyokushin karate.

Less than one percent of uchi-deshi who begin their training
will complete it. Those who do attain this accomplishment
are not only strong in the physical sense, but are mentally
strong as well. Over ninety-five percent of those individuals
who graduate from the program go on to receive their college
degrees. Their devotion to Kyokushin karate and Mas Oyama
is unquestionable. Their devotion to self-betterment and to
the betterment of others also goes without question. These
young men are accomplished, level-headed, and disciplined.
The following story relates the positive attributes and high-
ideals the uchi-deshi aspire to.

A first-year uchi-deshi, while involved in the 6:00 A.M. out-
door training session, was instructed by a senior instructor to
do push-ups for an infraction he committed. While in the
process of doing the push-ups the other uchi-deshi went on
their regular run. The single uchi-deshi continued his push-
ups. Returning to the honbu after their run the group of uchi-
deshi performed their stretches. Afterward they showered
and went to breakfast. It was not until a few hours later, during their regular karate session, that a senior instructor
inquired about the missing uchi-deshi. The others advised
that the last time they saw him he was outside doing push-
ups. When asked by the instructor as to why they did not
inform him that one of their own was missing, they replied
that a senior instructed the missing one to do push-ups and
it was not their place to question a senior. The instructor pro-

ceeded outside and found the uchi-deshi still doing push-ups
where the senior left him. When he was questioned as to
why he did not return to the honbu, he replied that he was
instructed by a senior to do push-ups, and if this meant all
day and night, he would do so. He went on to say that he
would not question a senior and he would not dishonor
Sosai Oyama, Kyokushinkai, or his fellow uchi-deshi by quitting his punishment.

The uchi-deshi are a formidable and important asset of the
Kyokushinkai. The training they experience is some of the
toughest in the martial arts world. They endure the hardship
of being away from their friends and family. At times they
become injured, yet they do not complain. They push themselves to the limits of human endurance. They do this
because they have chosen a path they know will make them
better human beings. They have chosen to follow not only the
technical path of Kyokushin karate, but to also adhere to the
mottoes and philosophies of its founder. They are the Young
Lions of Mas Oyama.

Chapter 9

Jissen Kumite
(Full-Contact Fighting)

Mas Oyama trained in many different methods of martial arts, taking from each the best he believed they had to offer. He instituted these various methods, along with his personal style, into what he established as Kyokushin karate. When Oyama founded Kyokushinkai, several styles of karate already existed in Japan. What set Kyokushin apart was not only its incorporation of the many different components of several styles, but also its intense training requirements that included physical contact without the use of protective equipment during kumite training. Oyama's idea of full, hard contact, as in classroom fighting, was at that time unheard of in karate. It was for certain not permitted during the practice of kumite in the other styles.

In the martial art of karate, kumite is regarded as the pinnacle of one's training. It is during kumite that the students of karate test their skills against one another. It is where the expression of karate's fundamental purpose—self-defense—is exhibited. Resembling a boxing match, two students face each other and on command move about delivering an assortment of techniques. There are many goals to be achieved from this form of training, and the students practice maneuverability, footwork, and adjusting the distance between themselves and their opponents. Students learn to block and avoid attacks. Various kicks and strikes, done singular or in combination, allow the student to acquire reactionary skills. The two primary goals of free fighting are the development of confidence and the ability to learn from one's mistakes.

In most styles of karate, including Kyokushin, many facets of training are required of a student before engaging in kumite. First, the student should be able to demonstrate a relative degree of proficiency in the basic blocks, kicks, and strikes. Second, the student should be familiar with the *bunkai* (practical application) of each kata and understand that kata is the bridge that spans the distance between *kihon* (basic techniques) and *kumite* (sparring). Finally, students should have practiced *renraku* (transitions), consisting of several combinations of blocks, kicks, and strikes executed in series while moving forward or backward across the floor.

Effective kumite requires the presence of three elements, which must come together in a compatible merger. These important elements are *cho shin* (body control), *cho soku* (breath control), and *cho shin* (mind control). The first, cho shin, requires that the body has a firm base (stance), from which it is easy to adapt and move. This requires that the body be flexible and that you maintain a suitable distance between you and the antagonist. Cho soku is the controlling of one's breathing. Breathing should be coupled with each movement. It should be slow and deep to prevent tension while reducing anxieties. The final element, the second cho shin, is, for many, the hardest. This is the control of the mind. When engaged in any form of combat, including kumite in the dojo, there is some degree of fear. One must learn to control these fears and use them to their benefit. Fear produces an increased flow of adrenaline. This increased flow of adrenaline should be manifested to energize the body and allow unconstrained movement. When these three elements come together, the fundamental purpose of karate—kumite in its correct form—will be realized.

Kumite is practiced with various degrees of difficulty and intensity. The most commonly recognized and most difficult and intense form is *jiyu-kumite*. Students engage each other in a format that is free flowing but with some restrictions placed on them. In most styles of karate, target areas on an opponent during kumite is limited to above the waist and techniques are restricted to the front of the body only. Moreover, some styles do not permit the head to be a target. The most common restriction is not to allow contact while

free fighting. In this case, students are expected to demonstrate control of their techniques by stopping them just short
of contact with their opponent. Many styles require that the
students wear protective equipment during free fighting.
In Kyokushin, jiyu-kumite is practiced with much fewer
restrictions. First, Kyokushin students do not rely on protective equipment. Second, target areas include the legs and
head. Finally, students are allowed to make contact.

Many students who practice karate do not like jiyu-kumite for
obvious reasons. This dislike can be attributed to many factors. The first and most common reason is fear. There is fear
of the unknown, fear of what to expect, and fear of getting
hurt. Everyone at one time or another during their life has
been injured. We associate injuries with pain. No one likes
pain. Therefore, the fear is not the injury itself, but the pain
associated with it. Second are the repercussions that come
with an injury, such as possibly not being able to go to work
or attend school the next day or worrying one's spouse. These
are legitimate concerns, as they should be. Another reason
some students do not like fighting is the act of fighting itself.
We live in a somewhat civilized society. Although Hollywood
and the media glamorize violence and fighting, that does not
change the basic feelings people have about fighting. The
physical act of fighting is discouraged by society. However,
karate is a martial art designed for self-protection and most
people who begin training in karate do so for the purpose of

learning self-defense. When a student learns how to fight, they should also be learning ways to avoid a fight. Once a student has learned to cope with and learn from their fears and misconceptions about fighting, they can then concentrate on proper fighting methods for practical, realistic self-defense.

Students should not participate in any form of kumite until they have a basic proficiency in kihon and kata. Their introduction to kumite should be at the lowest level. It should not be intense or difficult and it should have a minimal propensity for injury. As a student's ability and proficiency increases, then a higher level of kumite can be introduced. This step-by-step progression continues through all levels of kumite up to jiyu-kumite. By then, skill, confidence, and proficiency should enable the student to engage appropriately in free fighting—jiyu-kumite.

Kumite is learned in the same format as all other applications of karate are learned, beginning slowly with basic movements and gradually building to those that are more complex. The following represents the order of progression for kumite training in Kyokushin karate: *sanbon-kumite, ippon-kumite, kihon-kumite, yakusoku-kumite, tanshiki-kumite,* and finally jiyu-kumite. The following pages explain the definition and application of each form of kumite, which necessarily involves the participation of two students.

Sanbon-kumite (three-step fighting): The students face each other usually in *kumite dachi* (fighting stance) or *zenkutsu dachi* (front stance). One student is designated *tori* (attacker), the other, *uke* (defender). Tori is instructed to use a specific offensive technique. In turn, uke is instructed to use a specific block. On the command *"hajime"* (start/begin), tori advances toward uke, executing his technique. Uke moves away from the attack in the direction the instructor has set. As tori continues his

Jissen kumite (full contact fighting)

advance three times in succession, uke moves and defends against each advance. At the completion of the third advance, uke will counterattack. The roles are then reversed and the advancement and defense continues for another three movements, thus the name sanbon-kumite.

Ippon-kumite (one-step fighting): Tori and uke face each other just as in sanbon-kumite. The difference here is that tori only advances one time and uke moves back, defends, and counters against the attack all at once.

Kihon-kumite (basic-technique fighting): Here students work without partners, as they are instructed to use a sequence of blocks, strikes, and kicks in a prearranged combination. The students execute the combination of techniques from a fighting stance. They will execute the series several times over, each time on the command from the instructor. The kihon-kumite drills continue, with the combinations varying. During this training, the stances are mobile and the hands are in a position to the front of the body and not drawn back alongside the ribs like they are during kihon practice from a stationary stance. This hand position is more practical and allows for a quicker defense of the body and face.

Yakusoku-kumite (predetermined fighting): This is another drill that requires the use of a partner and pre-arranged techniques. Students are instructed as to what series of offensive and defensive techniques are to be utilized. On the order to begin, one student attacks with the specific offensive techniques. The other student reacts fast and attempts to defend each attack with the pre-determined blocks. Example: tori attacks with a *migi mae-geri* (right front kick), followed with a *hidari mawashi-geri* (left roundhouse kick), which is followed by a *migi ushiro-geri* (right back kick) that completes the series. Uke blocks with a variety of techniques to determine which ones are more effective against specific attacks. This exchange continues with each student alternating between offense and defense. The drill is done fast, but with the exchange of techniques being controlled. This exercise also teaches proper distance between opponents while developing reflexive actions.

Tanshiki-kumite **(limited technique fighting)**: This is another form of fighting that uses a partner and prearranged techniques. In this exercise, the techniques are limited by the instructor. For example, the offensive student may only kick, while the defending student may only block using the hands. The drill may be limited further by restricting the offensive technique to one specific kick or strike. For example, the attacker is restricted to the use of mae-geri (front kick) only, while the defending student can move about trying various blocks against the kick. The roles are then reversed. The same thing may be done with the attack limited to a specific hand strike. This exercise teaches control, footwork, and proper distancing while reducing the chances of injury.

Jiyu-kumite **(free fighting)**: This involves two students engaging each other in a somewhat restricted sparring match. Here the students do not use prearranged techniques or combinations. They are encouraged to throw a multitude of techniques in any series of combinations of their own choosing. These techniques are to be delivered to various areas of the body that have been deemed legitimate targets. A jiyu-kumite match could last several minutes depending on the instructor. During the match some styles may utilize a point system to qualify and quantify techniques delivered. A running tally of points may be used throughout the match without interruption to the fighters. The instructor may elect to interrupt the match each time a technique earns a score to advise the students. The match is then resumed again until the time of the match expires. The instructor may also elect *not* to use a scoring system. This allows the students the opportunity to fight without any interruptions and without the worries of who is winning and who is losing.

The exercise of kumite is a viable training tool. It assists the student in developing coordination, speed, agility, and motor skills. If utilized properly, kumite can help develop and enhance a student's confidence. It can also enhance the student's awareness of his training and teach how to learn from mistakes.

Mas Oyama believed in the benefits derived from the practice of kumite. However, he did not agree that the benefits were as all-powerful as did other karate instructors of his day. Oyama examined the various forms of kumite that each style of karate offered. He dissected each one, taking it apart bit by bit. He tested the various kumite techniques and applications of the other styles against his own students. After a long and careful analysis, Oyama came to a conclusion about kumite: something was missing. This missing element, he believed, was physical contact.

Oyama then considered other martial arts; that is, those other than karate. What he saw was *contact*. He observed that in ju-jutsu, practitioners utilize grabs, holds, throws, and joint-manipulations against each other. Without contact, they would be unable to apply their techniques. The same is true in judo, aikido, sumo, and kendo. They all use contact to move or defeat their opponent.

Oyama began incorporating into Kyokushin the element of contact that other karate styles lacked. Oyama's intense training regimen was fashioned after his own training developed years earlier in the mountains. Such training had one purpose: to condition the mind and body to its fullest. In the beginning, injuries due to the contact were sustained during training sessions. But as the students' physical conditioning became stronger, injuries waned. The decrease in injuries was not only because of their strength, but also because the students were becoming more effective in their blocking and evading abilities. This contact training by Oyama and his students influenced the development of full-contact no pads fighting (jissen-kumite) that was exclusive to Kyokushin.

Jissen-kumite is, in effect, jiyu-kumite (free fighting), but with two exceptions. First, in jissen-kumite, the opponents make full contact with one another. Second, the opponents are without any form of protective apparatus. To Oyama, his form of fighting was more realistic and applicable to self-defense scenarios than the non-contact fighting employed by the other karate styles. Many of the instructors from other karate styles condemned the full-contact style of fighting utilized by Oyama. They accused Oyama of sabotaging time-honored traditions of the art. Oyama viewed these accusations as nonsense. He knew the real reason as to why they objected to his ways of training and fighting. The tradition in question was of the mystique shrouding the art of karate. And the fear was that Oyama would expose that there was no mystique.

Oyama trained in the Shotokan and Gojo-ryu systems of karate. In these styles, contact is not permitted during kumite. Students of these styles are taught to halt their blows just inches from reaching their intended targets. Students are inundated with reasons as to why contact is not permitted. One such reason is that by stopping the technique just short of impact, it demonstrates that the student has mastered the technique and the ability to control it, and that if warranted the student would be able to follow through with the technique, thus incapacitating his opponent. The notion implied that the student's techniques were so powerful that contact could not be allowed. If contact did occur, ensuing results would be devastating. Students were further led to believe that they could execute a perfect technique at anytime and that the technique would inflict serious injury or even death.

Oyama heard many reasons throughout his training. He did believe there were some karateka who could injure or even kill with their techniques. However, he did not believe that all students of karate possessed this ability. To imply that all students possessed this devastating ability was absurd. Thus, Oyama accused these other instructors of misleading their students.

In the jissen-kumite of Kyokushin karate there are few restrictions. Techniques not permitted are limited to three: gouging of the eyes, direct attacks to the joints, and groin strikes. All other areas of the body are considered viable targets. Take-downs, sweeps, and throws are also permitted.

In the years to come, Oyama would take jissen-kumite one step further. In 1975, Oyama staged the First Kyokushinkai World Tournament in Tokyo, Japan. The format for this tournament was and still is jissen-kumite. Because of the intense training methods, comprehensive advancement (rank) requirements, and jissen-kumite, Kyokushin became known in Japan as "The Strongest Karate."

Chapter 10

Hyakunin Kumite
(100-Man Fighting)

Oyama's extensive knowledge of the martial arts reached far beyond the technical aspect. He was an avid reader with an insatiable appetite to acquire as much knowledge as he could about the martial arts. This passion for knowledge drove him to seek out anything published on the subject. However, he was not satisfied with just reading about the arts. He would visit dojos that practiced the various systems he was reading about. This allowed him a better understanding of the philosophies as well as the methodology behind each art. This thorough investigation of the Asian martial arts taught Oyama many things. One of the many things Oyama learned was that all the arts had something in common. This commonality was a supreme test of strength and endurance and only one out of the many hundreds of students in each art who attempts such a test is triumphant. This victory placed the student in a position of remarkable achievement, one that was respected and

admired by all students of their art. Oyama knew that such a
test was necessary for Kyokushinkai.

The test Oyama visualized for Kyokushinkai would require
far more than technical proficiency. It would demand that the
individual who accepted the challenge be at the peak of his
abilities. Physical endurance, strength, and mental stamina
would have to be tantamount. Physiological functions would
have to be at their peak. Kokoro—heart, mind, and body—
would have to be united as one.

Oyama chose *hyakunin-kumite* (100-man fighting) as the ultimate test for Kyokushin students. His decision to use
hyakunin-kumite came after careful study of other martial arts
and what they employed as their ultimate test. A nineteenth
century kenjutsu master, Yamoka Tesshu, performed
hyakunin-tachi, or "100 man challenge." Yamoka Tesshu, in
one hundred consecutive duels, victoriously fought opponents
with the *shinai* (bamboo sword). Mashiko Kimura stands
alone as the predominant athlete in judo, for no other practitioner of the art has ever accomplished the *hyakunin-nage,* or
"100-man throws." As friends, Oyama admired Kimura for his
intense training methods which were similar to Oyama's. Over
a period of two consecutive days, Kimura accomplished the
hyakunin-nage. These two 100-man fighting ordeals were the
factors in Oyama's choice of hyakunin-kumite for Kyokushin's
ultimate test.

Oyama would not require anything of his students that he himself had not previously done. Therefore, Oyama would elect to undertake the 100-man fighting first. It was soon after his arduous training in the mountains when Oyama chose hyakunin-kumite as the ultimate test for Kyokushin. Oyama was at the pinnacle of physical conditioning and believed there was no better time to take on such a task. Oyama selected the best black belt students from his dojo for his opponents. Oyama required each student to fight him for two minutes, consecutively. After the entire group of students fought Oyama they repeated their fighting rotation until one hundred bouts were complete. To satisfy Oyama's personal supreme test, he chose to face one hundred consecutive fights a day over the course of three days, for a total of three hundred fights. Oyama would take small breaks after every twenty or so fights in order to replenish fluids and tend to matters of personal hygiene. Sleep between each of the 100-man fight days was at a minimum for Oyama due to the increase of adrenaline and anticipation of the next day's fights.

Many of the students who faced Oyama fought three or four times during the three days. Several students could only face Oyama once due to injuries they sustained. Oyama would knock-out many students with a single blow. Oyama wanted to continue for a fourth day, but was unable to because of the lack of willing opponents. For these three days Oyama fought full-contact, without pads, against his top students, defeating them all. No other martial artist in history has even made an attempt at duplicating Oyama's three hundred-man fight. And because of the punishing effect this ordeal had on his students, Oyama would not attempt such a feat again. Oyama would now implement hyakunin-kumite into Kyokushin, as its ultimate test.

Oyama chose not to make hyakunin-kumite mandatory for his students. He wanted this test to be voluntary. Oyama believed that the voluntary status would add to the significance of such an ordeal because, by volunteering, the student would be demonstrating the true spirit of osu.

The first student of the Kyokushin organization to volunteer for the 100-man fighting ordeal was Steve Arneil. Arneil was a long-time student of Oyama who, for several years, lived in Japan while training at the honbu. The relationship between Oyama and Arneil was much more than just teacher and student. Many times Arneil would say that Oyama was like a father to him. To Arneil, taking this challenge was an honor. He did not want to let his mentor and father figure down.

In 1965 at the age of thirty, Arneil would encounter the hyakunin-kumite of Kyokushin karate. Over the course of two consecutive days he battled one hundred of Oyama's top students. Arneil triumphed and went down in the history of Kyokushinkai as the first to successfully complete the 100-man fights.

After Arneil successfully completed the 100-man kumite, Oyama asked him to go to Great Britain and assist the Kyokushin karate instructors that were already there. Representatives of Kyokushin teaching in Great Britain at the time were Bob Boulton, Bruce Donn, T. Sazuki, Kanazawa, and Enoeda. A collaborative effort on all their parts resulted in the formation of the British Karate Kyokushinkai (BKK). Bruce Donn became the first chairman of the newly formed BKK.

As one of the original founders of the BKK, Arneil eventually became chairman of the organization. However, his authority and teaching was confined by Mas Oyama to his own dojo. After much deliberation, Arneil, wanting to expand the BKK, resigned from the parent organization of Kyokushinkai under Oyama. Now he would be able to promote Kyokushin throughout all of Great Britain.

While chairman of the BKK, Arneil built the organization into one of the largest of the Kyokushin style outside of Japan. He is now chairman of the International Federation of Karate with affiliates throughout the world. He is an eighth level black belt in Kyokushin karate with the title of *hanshi* (master). Hanshi is a title that signifies the complete understanding of a specific martial art. It is given only to the highest of black belt ranks.

Five months after Arneil's successful hyakunin-kumite, the second attempt at Kyokushin's incomparable ordeal was made. This time the task would be undertaken by Tadashi

Nakamura. This was not Nakamura's first test to prove himself with the Kyokushinkai. Only one year earlier, in 1964, Nakamura went to Thailand to accept the challenge of the Thai boxers. Nakamura was successful in Thailand, returning to Japan with the World Kickboxing title. Nakamura was a strong fighter within the Kyokushin honbu who's training began at a very young age under the auspices of Mas Oyama. Through Oyama's grueling training, Nakamura would become the youngest recipient of a Kyokushin black belt under Oyama. Nakamura would also become the second man to successfully complete the Kyokushin hyakunin-kumite.

Tadashi Nakamura went on to become the chief instructor at the Kyokushinkai honbu. Nakamura, at the bequest of Oyama, left Japan in 1966 and traveled to the United States to establish a Kyokushin karate school there. Nakamura would go on to build a large organization for Oyama not only in the United States, but throughout North America. Nakamura became chairman of the North American Kyokushin Karate Organization and remained in this position until 1976.

In November of 1975 the First World Kyokushin Karate tournament was held in Tokyo. Representatives of the Kyokushin organization from all over the world met in Japan for this monumental event. Nakamura was present, serving as one of the tournament's chief principals. However, Nakamura was unhappy with certain undisclosed occurrences that took place at the tournament and upon returning to his home in New York, agonized over what happened. His ultimate decision, based on the incidents at the tournament, was to leave the Kyokushinkai. In March of 1976, Nakamura resigned from the Kyokushin Karate Organization. He would go on to found the World Seido Karate Organization, headquartered in New York City.

The third man to attempt the hyakunin-kumite was Shigeru Oyama in the year 1966. Shigeru Oyama, no relation to Mas Oyama, was one of the most outstanding students of Kyokushinkai. He would succeed Tadashi Nakamura as the chairman of the North American Kyokushin organization. Also like Nakamura, Shigeru Oyama would resign from the Kyokushinkai and would go on to establish a separate organization, the World Oyama Karate Organization, also headquartered in New York City. Keeping with the established tradition, Shigeru Oyama was victorious in the hyakunin-kumite.

In 1967, two prominent members of Kyokushinkai attempted and succeeded at the hyakunin-kumite. The two were Loek Hollander of Europe and John Jarvis of New Zealand. Hollander and Jarvis would go on to become chairmen of Kyokushin karate in their respective regions. Both of these gentlemen built strong Kyokushinkai organizations outside of Japan.

The hyakunin-kumites of Arneil, Nakamura, Oyama, Hollander, and Jarvis were completed over the course of two days each. Each man fought fifty consecutive fights with fifty different fighters each day for a total of one hundred fights. Unlike previous ordeals where the same opponents fought two and three times, each opponent they fought was fresh and at the peak of his performance. It would not be until 1972 that another attempt at Kyokushin's hyakunin-kumite would take place.

After the successful hyakunin-kumite of Hollander and Jarvis, Mas Oyama would change the requirement for hyakunin-kumite. In the past the event was held over two days, with fifty consecutive fights scheduled for each day, the new requirement would be one hundred fights in a single day. Mas Oyama had fought one hundred men each day for three consecutive days, even wanting to continue for a fourth day, increasing the number of fights to an unknown total. One hundred men in one day was not unheard of, and it would therefore become the standard for hyakunin-kumite in Kyokushinkai.

Howard Collins of Great Britain had been a live-in student of Mas Oyama at the Kyokushin honbu in Japan and would become the first man to successfully complete the 100-man fights in a single day. Before going to Japan, Collins' experience in the martial arts was limited. What karate knowledge he did have was from reading and studying from a book by

Oyama. Collins went to Japan for the specific purpose of training with Oyama. Upon arriving in Japan, Collins had little money, did not know the language, and had no means of support. In addition, he did not know Oyama and Oyama did not know him. Collins did not even know if he would be permitted to train under Oyama. Collins' move to Japan was a huge undertaking for a man who only wanted to train in karate. What if he was denied permission to train in Kyokushin under Oyama? Collins did not even have the financial means for a return plane ticket.

Collins was accepted by Oyama as a student at the honbu. His live-in status allowed him the opportunity to pay for his training and board by working odd-jobs at the headquarters. When it was time for Collins to test for his first level black belt under Oyama, Collins failed. He was successful on his second attempt. Collins had already been witness to two failed attempts by others at the hyakunin-kumite and he trained diligently for two years in preparation for his own.

When the day arrived for the hyakunin-kumite, Collins felt strong. However, over the course of several fights his endurance began to dwindle. Several times he was asked if he wanted to quit, but Collins persisted and went on to become the first person to complete the hyakunin-kumite in a single day. The year was 1972. Howard Collins is now a seventh dan, as promoted by Mas Oyama. He resides in Sweden, where he instructs Kyokushin karate and travels throughout the world promoting Kyokushin as the technical advisor for the organization.

In 1973, Miyuki Miura of Japan became the next to success-fully complete the 100-man fight in one day. The ordeal of fighting one hundred, two minute, full-contact, no pads, consecutive fights in one day is tumultuous. The ordeal lasts approximately four hours, although the time to completion can be shorter if the challenger is lucky enough to dispose of opponents faster than the two-minute rounds.

Obviously, the individual attempting the test needs to be in excellent physical and mental condition. Miura recalls that several hours after completing the 100-man fight his entire body was swollen. He could place his thumb anywhere on his body and the swelling would rise up to the second knuckle. He recalled that for two days he required assistance when going to the bathroom because he was unable to bend on his own. The hyakunin-kumite is an extraordinary accomplish-ment, but not without extraordinary punishment.

Kyokushin's hyakunin-kumite would see others make their attempts over the next several years, but without success. There is some contention that these failures were due to the emphasis on training for full-contact tournaments to the exclusion of training for the hundred man fight. Mas Oyama had began staging full-contact tournaments in Japan in 1968. The thought was that by participating in and training for several tournaments each year, the students were not devoting ample time to conditioning the body for the hundred-man test. However, this is debatable since those participating in the tournaments must also be in top condition. The tournaments are full-contact like the hundred-man fights, without pads, and consist of several fights. It is more likely that the emphasis on tournaments was a way to gain additional exposure for Kyokushinkai by Oyama. The tournaments would produce more spectators than the 100-man fights and this exposure would prove a better way to attract new students into Kyokushin.

After a long absence of hyakunin-kumite successes, in 1986 Akiyoshi Matsui became the next individual to succeed. Matsui, in addition to his triumphant 100-man fight, has also been able to add several other victories to his resume. He was winner of the All-Japan Tournament two times and Grand Champion of the Fourth World Tournament in 1987.

The next success at the hyakunin-kumite came in 1987, at the hand of a Brazilian named Ademir de Costa. Then, in 1989, Kaiji Sempai of Japan succeeded in the test. This was followed by Akira Masuda of Japan in 1994. In 1995 two others who successfully completed the test, Francisco-Alves Fihlo of Brazil and Kenji Yamaki of Japan, were also opponents at the 1995 Fifth World Tournament in Japan. Both of these men fought several fights during the tournament, with the final match for Grand Champion pitting the two face-to-face. In the end, Fihlo would be second runner-up and Yamaki would be Grand Champion. These two remarkable Kyokushin students not only were victorious in the World Tournament, but also victorious in the hyakunin-kumite in the same year.

Many students of Kyokushin karate have made an attempt at the hyakunin-kumite. And many have failed. The preparation for such an undertaking is relentless. Challengers must train for years. No other test of any other art or sport is quite like the hyakunin-kumite. The punishment the body withstands throughout this trial is unlike anything experienced by those of other athletics. Only twelve individuals in all of Kyokushin history have been able to conquer the ultimate test. The hundred-man ordeal requires extreme fortitude and perseverance. The hyakunin-kumite of Oyama's Kyokushin karate is the essence of the spirit of osu.

Chapter 11

World Champions

By 1960, Oyama had built Kyokushinkai into an international organization with more than seventy branches in over a dozen countries. Foreign students traveled to Japan to train under Oyama and he began to envision a special event that would be a vehicle to bring Kyokushin students together from around the world. Oyama decided that such a vehicle would be a grand tournament, wherein students from all over the world could unite. Here they could demonstrate their karate skills against each other in a competitive setting. The format for the event would be jissen-kumite—full-contact, knockdown competition. While Oyama knew this would be an impressive venue through which to further the growth of Kyokushin karate, he also knew that such an undertaking would require extensive planning and preparation. Oyama decided to begin on a smaller scale and promote regional tournaments in Japan to test the waters before going on to an international event.

Various styles of karate were already promoting their tournaments throughout Japan. The fighting format at these venues was typical of their training, where opponents would engage each other with a barrage kicks and punches, stopping their techniques short of impact. Oyama believed that his Kyokushin style of full-contact fighting would prove much more interesting to the spectators.

In 1968 Oyama promoted his first local tournament in Japan. The event proved to be as exciting for the spectators as it was for the fighters. Oyama would continue to promote tournaments throughout Japan but he needed to build a loyal gathering of spectators if his dream of an international event would become a reality.

Oyama staged specific tournaments that would lead the way toward an international tournament. In 1970 he established the First All Japan Tournament, which continues to be held to this very day. He also established an annual weight category tournament, which is also still to this day held in Osaka, Japan. Each of these events continue to draw thousands of spectators each year. The popularity of full-contact karate in Japan is due to the efforts of Oyama.

Oyama's international event became a reality for Kyokushinkai in 1975. This premier international Kyokushin

Oyama at a tournament in Japan.

milestone would be known as The First World Open Karate Tournament.

The First World Open Karate Tournament was just as its name implied—a tournament event open to all martial art practitioners. Invitations were sent to all the various styles of karate in Japan. Organizations within the Chinese, Korean, and Okinawan systems also received invitations. Many of the various styles and organizations sent representatives. In all, one hundred and twenty-eight fighters, from thirty-six countries participated in The First World Open Karate Tournament.

This First World Open Karate Tournament took place over three consecutive days. During the course of the three days, opponents fought each other in elimination rounds. Using the full-contact, no-pads style of fighting—jissen-kumite, the innovation of Oyama—the action was a heart pounding experience for all who witnessed it. The jissen-kumite also proved all too consuming for many of the contestants. Fighters from the various styles that did not employ the full-contact method of fighting were easily eliminated by the Kyokushin fighters. Many of these fighters were overwhelmed and devastated by the onslaught. For many, this was their first experience at receiving actual strikes during kumite. Several of the students from the other styles were injured, demonstrating that the non-contact training methods of other styles were ineffective against the Kyokushin fighters. During this First World Open Karate Tournament, no fighter from any of the other styles advanced to the finals. The jissen-kumite of Kyokushinkai proved itself far superior to the other styles of fighting in Japan at that time.

To triumph over an opponent in jissen-kumite, one "simply" must knock-out his opponent with a legal technique or render him unable to continue. The guidelines and rules for this first world event were as follows:

Fighting Format: Full-contact, without the use of protective equipment.

Tameshiwari **(object breaking):** Employ the hands, elbows, and feet as a pre-requirement. Fighters have to break a minimum of three boards with a hand strike, an elbow strike, and a foot strike. If a contestant is unable to break the minimum three boards with each technique, they would not be permitted to continue on to the fighting. Fighters may elect to attempt an additional number of boards above the three board minimum. The number of boards broken and the competitor's weight is used in the event of a tie.

Target Areas: Face, head, front of body, and legs.

Illegal Techniques: Hand or elbow strikes to the face and head, any technique to the back of the body, attacks to the groin, and direct attacks to the knee cap.

Legal Techniques: Any hand, elbow, or foot technique to the torso, and any kick to the face, head, and legs.

Judging: Four corner judges and one center referee. Each corner judge is furnished two flags, one *shiro* (white) and one *aka* (red). The color of the flags coincide with a color sash worn by each fighter.

Oyama at a tournament in Rochester, New York.

Scoring: Any legal technique that renders an opponent unconscious will be awarded *ippon* (one point and the striker declared winner); any legal technique that knocks down and renders a fighter unable to continue is considered ippon and the striker declared winner; any legal technique that downs an opponent, but allows the fighter to resume will receive *waza-ari* (half point); if a fighter obtains two waza-ari over his opponent during the round he will be declared winner; if at the end of the first regulation round one fighter has only scored a single waza-ari he will be declared winner; if at the end of the regulation round and the two overtime rounds, a winner is not declared by the judges, a decision will be made based on the results of the tameshiwari (breaking). At the conclusion of the first, or any consecutive rounds, the center referee will call for a decision of the judges, if a minimum of three judges votes for the same fighter, that fighter is declared winner. If the decision is split evenly between the judges for the two fighters, the referee can break the tie and declare a winner with his added vote. A win by decision of the judges is *hantei*. Fighters will be assessed *chui* (warnings for fouls and infractions). It requires the decision of three judges to assess a chui or the center referee can assess a chui on his own. If a fighter receives *chui-ni* (two warnings) he receives *genten-ichi* (first penalty). If a fighter receives two genten-ichi he is disqualified *(shikkaku)*. A fighter can also be disqualified on the basis of *shai hoki* (failing to appear).

Rounds: The competition takes place in one, three minute round. If no winner is declared at the end of the first round a second round of two minutes would be required. If still no decisive winner has been declared, a third two minute round would be required. At the end of the two overtime rounds, if a decisive winner was not proclaimed by the judges, the number of boards broken and the weight of the fighter would break the tie. If the fighters broke the same number of boards, the win would go to the fighter who weighed less.

The martial arts place strong emphasis on the principles of discipline, respect, and proper protocol. Kyokushin karate adheres to these principles and requires the fighters and everyone involved in a tournament to do the same. While witnessing a Kyokushin tournament, one cannot help but notice the respect the fighters pay to the referee, judges, tournament director, and coaches. The same respect is obvious amongst the fighters to each other. Fighters do not argue a decision of the referee or judges. Contestants do not vent their anger and frustration over losing. Fighters do not strut throughout the arena while waiting their turn. Spectators do not block the views of others to the fighting area. Instead, order and respect for the art of Kyokushin karate is evident and exemplified everywhere.

Once the tournament director or supreme judge takes their position, the tournament commences. The first thing spectators notice is the way the four judges and referee approach the contestant area. The four judges walk in a single-file following the referee. The referee and each judge pause before entering the area and pay their respects to the supreme judge with *rei* (bow) and the voicing of osu. The five people then line-up facing the head table, bow, and say osu, then turn 180 degrees to face the spectators and repeat the bow and osu. Again, they turn 180 degrees to again face the head table, then move individually to their respective corners.

At each corner is a chair and a set of flags for each judge. The referee takes his position in the center of the contestant area or ring. Over the personal address system the names of the first two fighters are announced. Quickly, each fighter, along with his coach, reports to their corner of the ring. The corner of the ring determines the color sash that the fighter will wear during the fight, either red or white. Each fighter faces the head table and bows and says osu then proceeds to the center of the ring where the referee awaits. The referee ties the appropriate color sash to the back of the fighter's *obi* (belt).

Once this is completed the referee has the fighters face each other a few feet apart. On the command from the referee, *shomen ni rei* (bow to the front), the fighters face the head table and bow. The referee then has the fighters face him and on his command bow to the main judge and then to the referee. Next, the referee has the fighters face each other and on his command of *otagi ni rei* (bow to each other), the fighters pay their respect to one another.

The referee then gives the command *kamaete* (take fighting positions), and the fighters assume their stance, ready to begin. When the referee commands hajime (begin), the fighters immediately engage each other. If at anytime during the bout the referee wants the fighters to stop, he will shout *yame* (stop!). Fighters will immediately stop and face the judge for further instruction. When the referee is ready to resume the bout he will say *zokko* (start again).

At the end of the bout, if there has been no knockout or knockdown, the referee will line up the fighters so as to face each other. He then calls for the vote of the judges who signal their decision by raising one of the colored flags. A flag raised above the head signals a vote for victory of the fighter whose sash color matches the flag. A victory by decision requires the votes of three judges or two judges and the referee's concurrence. If a majority signals with their flags in a crossed position between their legs, the bout is declared a draw and the fighters must fight again. At the conclusion of a fight and declaration of a winner, the referee lines up the fighters in their original starting positions. He announces shomen ni rei and the fighters face the head table and bow, then the referee announces shushin ni rei and the fighters face him and bow. At the referee's command, otagi ni rei, the fighters face each other and bow, shake hands, and depart from the ring. As each fighter reaches their exit point of the contestant area, they stop and as a final token of their respect, face the head table and bow, and then proceed to leave the area. This protocol is repeated throughout the course of the tournament.

After The First World Open Karate Tournament, Mas Oyama would stage the tournament every four years. The setting for this event would be Tokyo, Japan. Each country participating in the tournament would send a five man team and one alternate with the airfares and accommodations for each Kyokushin chairman, the team, and the coach paid for by Oyama and the Kyokushinkai. To be chosen as a team member to represent your country was an honor and, for many, a once-in-a-lifetime opportunity. Now all a team member had to do was fight.

Oyama at a tournament in Japan.

Unlike one-day regional Kyokushin tournaments, there are no weight categories in the World Open. On the first day of competition contestants are issued a number. These numbers are affixed to the back of their dogi (uniform) top. All insignias or logos of the various styles that adorn the dogi are covered with tape. This is to prevent any bias among the judges. The contestants are then lined-up in pairs according to height for the first round of fighting. During the elimination rounds contestants who are victorious go on to fight again. The eliminations continue until there are four contestants who will fight for the third through first place and Grand

Oyama at the All-Japan Tournament

Champion positions on the final day of competition. Those individuals who advance to this point may have to fight as many as six to eight times over three days to reach the finals. Once again, these fights are full-contact, without pads. Each time a fighter steps into the ring he knows that his opponent is trying to knock him out. To be able to participate in such an event and advance to the finals requires an extraordinary amount of training and perseverance.

Within the Kyokushin organization there is the following saying; *"for every three minutes of jissen-kumite, one must train three thousand minutes."* Kyokushin karate training is intense and demanding. The duration of a typical Kyokushin training session is one-and-a-half to two hours. Throughout the training session students cover many aspects of Kyokushin karate. There is little down-time and the pace of the class is fast. A normal training session begins with a five-to-ten minute warm-up period. The warm-up consists of exercises that increase the blood-flow to the muscles and joints to help prevent their overexertion.

Following the warm-up phase is the practice of kihon—the fundamental blocks, kicks, strikes, and punches. For the next twenty-to-thirty minutes the students, following the lead of the instructor, usually execute a minimum of thirty repetitions of each basic technique. By the end of this portion of training, each student will have executed between nine hundred and twelve hundred repetitions. Mas Oyama used to say it was okay if the instructor did more than thirty repetitions for each technique, but never less. Because of the pace of kihon practice, the heart rate accelerates to produce an aerobic result and increased cardiovascular endurance.

Ido-geiko (moving training) begins immediately after kihon practice. During ido-geiko, students move across the floor in different stances, while executing the various blocks, kicks, strikes, or combinations thereof. The instructor varies the pattern of movement during ido-geiko. Students may find themselves moving forward to a five-count repetition, then turn and repeat, or they could find themselves facing forward but moving backwards, tracing their preceding movements.

Kata, the formal exercise practice, or sanbon, or ippon-kumite will follow ido-geiko. Usually the final segment of training before the cool-down period is when kumite (fighting) is done.

The instructor may vary the order of practice from class to class or may chose to eliminate one aspect of training and add another. Instead of sanbon or ippon-kumite, pad drills or work on the suspended heavy-bags may be incorporated into the training sequence. Whatever the format, each class places physical as well as mental demands on all the students.

Those Kyokushin students who desire to compete in jissen-kumite tournaments undergo other training sessions in addition to their regular dojo training. The design of these additional sessions focus on specific areas of training. These specific areas include, but are not limited to: weight-resistance to increase strength, running or biking for cardiovascular endurance, suspended heavy-bag striking to increase strength, power, and endurance, fighting strategy, and sparring. Training in more than one discipline simultaneously is known as cross-training. Cross-training is essential for maximum performance in any athletic endeavor. All Kyokushin students should have a cross-training regimen of their own. Cross-training will enhance a student's performance in the dojo. Extensive knowledge and application of Kyokushin's training concepts and philosophies, along with the physical prowess of strength, power, flexibility, and endurance are essential qualities that help make a good fighter. However, to become a good fighter requires more than just physical attributes and knowledge.

To be a good fighter also requires a desire and mental capacity to persevere. If a fighter has some of these qualities, but lacks others, he will not succeed. Success depends on a combination of all these elements. Physical attributes and an unshakable desire and perseverance (the spirit of osu), are the distinct characteristics that make for a worthy advocate of jissen-kumite. A Kyokushin student who possesses these particular characteristics should set their sight on representing their country in the World Open Karate Tournament.

The First World Open Karate Tournament was a huge success. Tens of thousands of spectators packed the arena on each of the three days. At no other time has the karate world been witness to such a diverse mixture of international full-contact fighters. The caliber of the fighters was in keeping with an event of this magnitude—world class. They came from all over the world with an exuberance, a willingness to fight, and a sportsmanship that radiated throughout the tournament. What also was evident was the camaraderie of the participants. Social, religious, and ethnic stigmas that plague races and countries ceased to exist for the moment. Co-existence among the diverse cultures, religions, and races would thrive for the three days. Perhaps Sosai Oyama's dream of world-peace through Kyokushin karate was not that absurd. It was clear to all who were present that the fighters came to honor Sosai Oyama and demonstrate their Kyokushin karate skills. Each fighter would also have the honor of making history in Kyokushinkai as competitors in the First World Open Karate Tournament.

The First World Open Karate Tournament was barely over when plans for the second such event were set in motion. Since 1975, and every four years since, the city of Tokyo would play host to World Open Karate Tournament. There have been six such tournaments since those first three days in 1975.

World Open Kyokushin Karate Champions

Event	Year	Grand Champion	Country	Style
First World Open	1975	Katsuaki Sato	Japan	Kyokushin
Second World Open	1979	Makoto Nakamura	Japan	Kyokushin
Third World Open	1983	Makoto Nakamura	Japan	Kyokushin
Fourth World Open	1987	Akiyoshi Matsui	Japan	Kyokushin
Fifth World Open	1991	Kenji Midori	Japan	Kyokushin
Sixth World Open	1995	Yamaki—IKO 1	Japan	Kyokushin

After the death of Mas Oyama in 1994 the International
Karate Organization (IKO) of the Kyokushinkai in Japan split.
There are now three groups in Japan representing themselves
as IKO. They are known as IKO 1 under the direction of
Matsui, IKO 2 under the direction of Nishida, and IKO 3
under the direction of Masushima. In 1997, the IKO 2 held a
tournament known as The First World Cup. This event was a
weight-category type with three divisions for men and two
division for women. A Grand Champion for each of the five
divisions exist.

First World Cup, 1997

Division	Grand Champion	Country	Style
Women's Lightweight	Rita Sztanko	Hungary	Kyokushin
Women's Heavyweight	Roma Miksyte	Europe	Kyokushin
Men's Lightweight	Ko Tanigawa	Japan	Kyokushin
Men's Middleweight	Tadashi Ishihara	Japan	Kyokushin
Men's Heavyweight	Norichika Tsukamoto	Japan	Kyokushin

Both IKO 1 and IKO 2 are staging World Open Tournaments
in 1999. It is unknown at the time of this writing if there will
be three World Open Kyokushin Karate Tournaments in 1999.

Chapter 12

Kyokushinkai Ambassadors

Within the Kyokushinkai special titles and qualifications are given to the various levels of the black belt rank. First and second level black belts are qualified as *renshi*—time for developing one's own techniques and skills. Individuals of the first and second level black belt are addressed as sempai (senior). Individuals of the third and fourth level black belt are *kyoshi* (instructor) and are addressed as sensei (teacher). Individuals who are fifth level black belt or higher are qualified as hanshi (man of example). These individuals are addressed as shihan (dojo master). All of these ranks and qualifications are a necessary part of the hierarchy system within Kyokushinkai.

The designated system of hierarchy in Japan is *iemoto*. Iemoto is also the designated patriarch or leader of an organization. The iemoto has complete control over the traditions, resources, and articles of the organization. This patriarch also controls who will inherit the organization when he is gone. The hierarchy within the iemoto system involves close personal connections and brotherhood. Loyalty and trust are the requirements of such an association. Within this hierarchy system the sempai/kohai (senior-to-junior) relationship is without question. As the iemoto of Kyokushinkai, Mas Oyama governed all students and members and was the only one who could authorize promotions, issue certificates of rank, elevate one to instructor status, and appoint branch chiefs.

Branch chiefs are individuals who, during his lifetime, Oyama chose to spread the art of Kyokushinkai throughout the world. Branch chiefs are the only members who, on the authority of Oyama, were able to open and operate dojos. These senior members of the organization also have the authority to grade and promote students through the rank of nidan (second level black belt). Individuals seeking promotion to sandan (third level black belt) or higher must travel to the honbu in Japan for the grading exam. Branch chiefs oversee Kyokushin activities within a specific region in their respective countries. They may have several branch schools in their area under their responsibility. Black belt students of the branch chiefs may perform the instruction at these additional schools. Although they are of the black belt rank, these assistant instructors cannot issue rank themselves.

To be eligible for a position of branch chief, an individual must hold a minimum rank of sandan black belt in the organization. The individual must also have a minimum of three hundred students registered with the headquarters in Japan, as less than three hundred students is classified as a club by honbu. An individual must possess the ability to teach and explain the philosophies, as well as instruct the methods and techniques of Kyoklushin karate. Additional qualifications include: superior leadership abilities, a good personality, an understanding of the ideology of Kyokushin karate, strong management skills, and extensive training in Japan. The appointment of branch chief used to come directly from Mas Oyama. Branch chiefs are now appointed by the president of Kyokushinkai. The number of branch chiefs Oyama appointed for each country were few.

Branch chiefs of the Kyokushinkai make annual trips to Japan to attend special training camps. These training camps are attended only by branch chiefs and attendance at several consecutive annual training camps is one of the requirements for promotion to the next black belt level. Branch chiefs must also attend the World Open Kyokushin Karate Tournament that is held every four years in Japan. Branch chiefs must also hold an instructor qualification within Kyokushinkai. Individuals eligible for instructor status must successfully complete the fifty-man jissen-kumite. These are just some of the reasons why so few Kyokushinkai branch chiefs have been appointed. The position of branch chief in Kyokushinkai is a demanding one, requiring intricate knowledge of all the workings and philosophies of the organization in addition to possessing a high-level of skill, technical ability, and physical fitness. Most branch chiefs continue to instruct and workout side-by-side with their students well into their later years. The strength of Kyokushin karate continues because of these branch chiefs and the intense demands Oyama required of them and their dedication and loyalty.

Chapter 13

The Legacy

To many, Mas Oyama was bigger than life. Throughout his prime years, Oyama's exploits preceded him wherever he went. Until his death, Oyama was relentless in his pursuit of perfection in Kyokushin karate. A task master, Oyama demanded and received more than one-hundred percent from every soul who sought his guidance and instruction. He motivated and inspired those who came in contact with him. His students learned to dig deep within themselves to find their inner strength and to persevere to achieve their goals. Oyama personified karate his entire life—through his deeds, his relationships, his training, and his philosophy.

Below is a sampling of Oyama's many thoughts and philosophical insights:

> *"Although it is important to study and train for*
> *skill in techniques, for the man who wishes to truly*
> *accomplish the way of budo, it is important to make*

his whole life in training and therefore not aiming for skill and strength alone, but also for spiritual attainment."

"A human life gains luster and strength only when it is polished and tempered."

"Reading good books implants good ideas in the mind, develops good aspirations, and leads to the cultivation of good friends."

"One living daily in the Way carries their head low and their eyes high; reserved in speech and possessing a kind heart, they steadfastly continue in their training efforts."

"Aspirations must be pure and free of selfishness. Arising from the depths of the soul, aspirations are spiritual demands penetrating all of a human life and making it possible for a person to die for their sake. A person without aspirations is like a ship without a rudder or a horse without a bridle. Aspirations give consistent order to life."

"As far as possible, I want nothing more than to don my training gi and teach karate."

"If someone asked me what a human being ought to
devote the maximum of his life to, I would answer:
training. Train more than you sleep."

"Karate is the most Zen-like of all the martial arts.
It has abandoned the sword. This means that it
transcends the idea of winning and losing to become
a way of thinking and living for the sake of other
people in accordance with the way of Heaven.
Its meanings, therefore, reach the profound levels
of human thought."

"One must try everyday to expand one's limits."

"Behind each triumph are new peaks to be
conquered."

"Until the day I die, I never want to be separated
from my dogi; I never want to cease my training
efforts in the dojo."

"The fastest way to attain courage is to follow the
chosen Way and be willing to abandon life itself
for the sake of justice."

"If you have confidence in your own words, aspira-
tions, thoughts, and actions and do your very best,
you will have no need to regret the outcome of what
you do. Fear and trembling are the lot of the person
who, while stinting effort, hopes that everything will
come out precisely as he wants."

"Human beings are capable of virtually limitless
degradation; they are also capable of virtually
limitless improvement and achievement. Success
depends on goals and on diligence in pursuing
them."

"Always remember that the true meaning of budo is
that soft overcomes hard, small overcomes large."

"The most significant life is the one lived on the
basis of a personal sense of justice and the desire
to see justice realized everywhere."

"Is it possible for even the smallest of accolades of
achievement to be truly worthwhile without tears
and toil?"

"I realized that perseverance and step-by-step
progress are the only ways to reach a goal along
a chosen path."

Oyama performing kanku at Niagara Falls.

*"Subjecting yourself to vigorous training is more
for the sake of forging a resolute spirit that can
vanquish the self than it is for developing
a strong body."*

*"Each of us has his cowardice. Each of us is afraid
to lose, afraid to die. But hanging back is the way
to remain a coward for life. The way to find courage
is to seek it on the field of conflict. And the sure way
to victory is willingness to risk one's own life."*

*"We in Kyokushin maintain faith in a Way that
knows no prejudices."*

*"My Way is the Way of karate, which is also the
Way of humanity, and which is consequently related
to the Way of Heaven."*

*"A man who understands decorum and the courte-
sies is a great treasure; I hope to train and send into
society as many such men as I can."*

*"No matter how strong the rival, the just will
always win."*

*"True courage is born only when it is accompanied
by justice."*

"Courtesy should be apparent in all our actions and words and in all aspects of daily life. But by courtesy, I do not mean rigid, cold formality. Courtesy in the truest sense is selfless concern for the welfare and physical and mental comfort of the other person."

"The Kyokushin karate organization is unique. It is vital that we honor the qualities that make our karate budo karate."

"For me, tranquil absorption the Zen priest finds in seated meditation is replaced by the total absorption I experience in exhausting karate training. Bathed in sweat, devoted entirely to what I am doing, in training sessions I transcend both life and death."

"Karate is budo and if the budo is removed from karate it is nothing more than sport karate, show karate, or even fashion karate—the idea of training merely to be fashionable."

"I have not permitted myself to be ignorant of any martial art that exists. Why? Such ignorance is a disgrace to someone who follows the path of the martial arts."

*"If you do not overcome your tendency to give
up easily, your life will lead to nothing."*

*"Since karate exists for cultivating the spirit and
training the body, it must be a moral way surpassing
mere technique. . . ."*

*"In the martial arts, introspection begets wisdom.
Always see contemplation on your actions as an
opportunity to improve."*

*"Power is no more than a part, no more than the
tip of the iceberg of the limitless profundity and
sublimate of karate."*

*"Studying the martial Way is like climbing a cliff:
keep going forward without rest. Resting is not
permissible because it causes recessions to old
adages of achievement. Persevering day in, day
out improves techniques, but resting one day
causes lapses. This must be prevented."*

*"Personal greed and egoism are the things that
cause human beings to forget respect for others and
to violate rules that have been established for the
sake of peace and friendship."*

"Come ye trials and challenges; come life's big waves, for I am ready!"

April 26, 1994 is the most significant date in the history of Kyokushinkai. For on this date the founder and leader of Kyokushin karate, Mas Oyama, passed away. Mas Oyama, the man, is gone. However, his spirit exists in every Kyokushin dojo throughout the world and in the heart of every Kyokushin student. The legend may be gone, but his legacy continues . . .

Chronology of Mas Oyama and Kyokushinkai

1923

Masutatsu Oyama was born in South Korea.

1925

Oyama was sent by his parents to his sister's house in Manchuria.

1936

Oyama entered primary school in Seoul, Korea, where he started his study of Chinese kempo. In his second year he gained shodan.

1938

Oyama entered Yamanshi Airways School, Japan.
  Oyama studied karate under Gichin Funakoshi.

1940

Oyama entered Takushoki University.
  Gained karate second dan.

1945

Oyama started the Eiwa Karate-Do Research Institution in Suginami-ku.

1946

Oyama entered the Physical Education Department of Wascda University.
  Oyama visited Eiji Yoshikawa and Shiro Ozaki, famous writers, to study the old samurai way. Oyama went to Mt. Minobu for training.

1947
Oyama entered the First All Japan Tournament since the war and reigned champion.

1948
Oyama devoted his life to karate and trained alone for eighteen months on Mt. Kiyosumi in Chiba.

1950
Oyama fought and defeated his first bull.

1952
Oyama traveled to the United States, giving exhibitions and accepting challenges for nearly a year. He was undefeated.

1953
Oyama traveled to United States again and fought a bull in Chicago.
Opened first dojo in Mejiro, Tokyo.

1956
The true start of the Oyama Dojo behind Rikkyo University.

1957
The first Kyokushin karate dojo outside of Japan was opened in Hawaii by Bobby Lowe.

1958
Oyama's *What is Karate* was published, becoming the first best-selling book on Japanese karate.
The FBI in Washington, D.C. and the U.S. Army at Westpoint invited Oyama to the U.S. to teach them his karate.

1959

The first Hawaii tournament was held, Oyama attended
as chief judge.

The Oyama Dojo held its first Summer Training School.

1960

Seventy-two Branches of Kyokushin karate were started
in 16 countries.

1961

San Francisco and Los Angeles dojos opened.

Oyama attends the First North American Tournament
held in Madison Square Garden, New York.

1963

Construction started on the Kyokushinkaikan honbu
in Ikebukuro, Tokyo.

1964

Thai boxing challenge accepted and won.

E. Sato (former Prime Minister of Japan), who had
recently won the Nobel Prize, became the President
of the Kyokushinkaikan and Oyama was given the title
of kancho (director). I.K.O. was established and the Tokyo
honbu officially opened.

1965

Winter training on Mt. Mitsumine was held for the first time.
Oyama's *This is Karate* was published and became known
as the so-called "Bible of Karate."

Steve Arneil of Britain became the first student of
Kyokushin to win the 100-man kumite.

1966

Oyama published *Dynamic Karate* (Jpn.). Shigeru Oyama was sent to the U.S.

Sean Connery of 007 fame trained in Japan and became a member of the board.

S. Oyama won the 100-man kumite.

1967

Oyama published *Vital Karate*.

L. Hollander of Holland and J. Jarvis of New Zealand achieved the 100-man kumite.

1969

Oyama's *Boys Karate, Karate for the Millions,* and *Young Man's Karate Self-Defense* were published.

The first Japan Open Tournament was held.

1970

Oyama's *Advanced Karate* was published.

1971

The USA main branch was established in Manhattan, New York. Oyama attended the meeting with Mayor Lindsay.

1972

Yusuhito Oyama was sent to the U.S. to teach karate there.

H. Collins of Britain achieved the 100-man kumite. The first to accomplish this in a single day.

1973

Miyoki Miura achieved the 100-man kumite.

1974

Oyama was presented with 9th dan from Japan.

1975

The First World Open Tournament was held in Tokyo, 128 competitors from thirty-six countries attended.

1976

The first two volumes of Oyama's *The Strongest Karate* were released.

1977

The English quarterly magazine *Kyokushin-Karate* was started, and the monthly Japanese magazine *Power Karate* was published by the honbu.

1978

The first European Kyokushin tournament was held in London.

1979

Three men attempted 100-man kumite, but were unsuccessful.

The 2nd World Open Tournament was held in Tokyo.

1980

Oyama traveled to the United States and Canada instructing at various dojos.

The twelfth All-Japan Open Karate Tournament is held.

1981

Mas Oyama interviewed for *GQ* magazine.

The First South American Kyokushin Tournament was held in Brazil.

The thirteenth All Japan Open Karate Tournament was held.

1982

The Australian Kyokushin Open Karate Tournament
was held.

1983

The First Sri Lanka Kyokushin Open Tournament was held.
   Five thousand people gathered to celebrate the twentieth
anniversary of Kyokushin karate.
   The Prince of Nepal visited and trained at the honbu.

1984

The Third World Open Tournament was held.
The First All Japan Open Weight Tournament was held
in Osaka.

1985

Mr. More, Chairman of the IKO, dies.

1986

Seiji Isobe was sent to Brazil to establish Kyokushin in South
America.

1987

The Fourth World Open Karate Tournament was held.

1988

The United Kingdom Open Karate Tournament was held in
Sydney to celebrate the anniversary of Australia. Mas Oyama
attends and demonstrates.

1989

Mas Oyama lectures to International Olympic Committee
members.

1990

A World Branch Chief conference and training was held
in Japan.

1991

The Far Eastern Siberian Branch of Kyokushinkai was
established.

   The Fifth World Open Tournament was held.

1992

Oyama attends the American International Karate
Tournament in Rochester, NY. This was his last trip
to the United States.

1993

Mas Oyama receives his tenth dan from Japan.

1994

April 26th—The founder of Kyokushin karate, Sosai Mas
Oyama, dies.

References

Ligo, N. (1994). *Budo Karate Illustrated '94.* USA: Author.

Oyama, M. (1958). *What is Karate?* Tokyo: Shuppansha Publications.

Oyama, M. (1973). *This is Karate.* Tokyo: Japan Publications.

Oyama, M. (1979). *Advanced Karate.* Tokyo: Japan Publications.

Oyama, M. (1979). *The Kyokushin Way.* Tokyo: Japan Publications.

About the Author

Michael J. Lorden is a branch chief-instructor for the Kyokushin Karate Organization of Tokyo, Japan. His association and experience in karate exceeds thirty-nine years. In addition to his karate experience, Lorden holds certifications in defensive tactics from the FBI and the U.S. Military. His twenty-eight years as an operative and instructor in military and law enforcement special operations has earned him an extensive and interesting insight into this unique environment. His certified instructor status includes firearms, anti-terrorism, hostage rescue, tactical and evasive driving, rappelling, PR-24 baton, ASP baton, physical fitness specialist, as well as other specialized areas of high-risk special operations. Mr. Lorden is a court certified expert in defensive tactics, chemical agents, and high-risk tactical operations. He holds a BS in business

Author in fighting posture.

management. He is a graduate of the ISC Division of Wellness (Fitness Specialist—Physical Wellness Planner).

Mr. Lorden is a published writer of several articles and newsletters, as well as a book on law enforcement defensive tactics. He is a full-time writer, as well as Kyokushin karate instructor. As a branch chief for the International Kyokushin Karate Organization he insures their philosophies and training requirements are up to standard in the United States. He currently resides in Colorado Springs, Colorado, with his wife Jennifer, where they own and operate their Kyokushin dojo.